RETR PRACTICE: PRIMARY

A guide for primary teachers and leaders

KATE JONES

First Published 2022

by John Catt Educational Ltd,
15 Riduna Park, Melton, Woodbridge, Suffolk IP12 1QT
01394 389850
enquiries@johncatt.com
www.johncatt.com

Tel: +44 (0) 1394 389850
Fax: +44 (0) 1394 386893
Email: enquiries@johncatt.com
Website: www.johncatt.com

ISBN: 978 1 915261 20 5

Set and designed by John Catt Educational Limited

An evidence-informed approach to teaching and learning is efficient and effective as well as thoroughly enjoyable. I refer to this passion and desire to become an evidence-informed teacher and an obligation to challenge outdated and debunked neuromyths, as the 'Kirschner effect'.

Dedicated to Professor Paul A. Kirschner.

Thank you for everything you have taught me and the support you have provided to help move the teaching profession forward.

PRAISE FOR RETRIEVAL PRACTICE: PRIMARY

We all know that how we help children know and remember is a key part of learning, but we also know that there is more to learning than that. Kate strikes a wonderful balance to help us help children to remember the important things, but she doesn't lose sight of the more-ness and the special that is also a fundamental part of primary education. A great book; practical, purposeful and definitely primary.

**Simon Smith, primary principal at
The Enquire Learning Trust. @smithsmm**

Kate's thorough and accessible review of the research and evidence for retrieval practice in primary schools is a must read. The book highlights the vital role of retrieval practice in learning for even the youngest children and is full of practical ideas about how it can be implemented in the primary classroom from EYFS onwards. This book is essential reading both for those new to the idea of retrieval practice as well as those who wish to refine their current practice.

**Tarjinder Gill, associate director of research and pedagogy,
Outwood Grange Academies Trust. @teach_well**

There is always a never-ending stack of more plates to spin and balls to juggle in education and as a headteacher, deciding on which area to prioritise is just one of many. I've been looking at retrieval practice and how we can encourage children to recall learning quickly and effectively, and Kate's work has been so helpful in this. With worked examples, clear explanations and valuable links, this book is going to provide the team with the help we need to get children to be retrieval experts.

Ben Waldram, primary headteacher. @mrwaldram

Kate has written a book that is rooted in research and still accessible to classroom teachers. The way it's written cleverly weaves together the theoretical principles and what actually goes on in a classroom which makes it so user-friendly. I have a long list of takeaways that I want to embed in my teaching and when writing resources for others. It's a brilliant read which primary teachers should add to their bookshelves! Heartily recommend!

Stuart Tiffany, teacher and CPD provider. @mr_s_tiffany

This book was worth the wait. Kate Jones possesses a true gift in making theory practical and directly applicable in the classroom. The book gives the beginner a clear image of what retrieval practice is (and what it isn't) and a solid base to start using it right away. In this book the expert will find new insights and many more ways to apply retrieval practice effectively at every moment in every lesson. The slogan 'because, you're worth it' is absolutely true for this book. Both you and your students will be enjoying *Retrieval Practice Primary.*

Debbie Dussel, teacher of primary education in the Netherlands

Any book that tries to bridge the gap between research and classroom experience is essential reading. That Kate has managed to combine carefully curated research with practical, actionable advice and examples, in a way that makes it accessible for time-poor teachers, makes it all the more worthwhile a read.

Kieran Mackle, primary mathematics specialist/collaboration lead. Author of *Thinking Deeply about Primary Mathematics.* @Kieran_M_Ed

This book is a brilliant resource for primary teachers at any stage in their career. It is a perfect blend of research evidence and practical advice. If you want to really get going with retrieval practice or are looking for new ideas, this book is what you need. You could put the ideas from the book into practice tomorrow without adding to your workload.

Bryn Goodman, teacher of Year 5, South Failsworth Primary School. @bryngoodman

In primary schools, we have always been aware of our pupils' abilities to encode and store huge amounts of information. Just ask any five-year-old about their favourite dinosaurs. Yet, engaging with research and theory about retrieval practice could sometimes be overwhelming. Not in this book. Kate opens up the evidence in an engaging way and packs in valuable case studies, references for further reading, and plenty of practical takeaways. It perfectly balances the rigour of the most relevant research with a recognition of the wonderful uniqueness of every primary setting. This is a book to return to again and again as you explore its ideas in the context of your classroom.

**Nathan Gynn, alternative curriculum co-ordinator,
Pentrehafod School. @lessoncopy**

We know that retrieval practice can have a profound impact on pupils' learning and Kate Jones has written the book that primary teachers and leaders need to make the most of this powerful approach. With a clear focus on practical application, Kate describes how schools can maximise the opportunities for retrieval practice and how to avoid the common pitfalls that beset schools. It's evidence-informed, accessible and full of concrete examples and case studies that will ensure schools are able to unlock the power of retrieval practice. Whether you are completely new to retrieval practice or simply want to develop your existing practice further, this is an essential read.

**Andrew Percival, deputy headteacher at
Stanley Road Primary School, Oldham. @primarypercival**

This is a fantastic read for leaders and staff alike. Kate has made us aware of the limitations of working memory and what we can do to take steps to help children so they can be successful learners in the primary classroom. This book has also helped encourage dialogue with the staff team when planning and designing our new curriculum going forward. I would definitely recommend it!

**Sarah Hutchinson, headteacher,
St Cuthbert's RC Primary School, Carlisle. @sarahhutcho207**

Kate has written a book that is evidenced-informed and instantly accessible. She takes apart retrieval practice to develop practical, low-effort yet sustainable approaches that can become part of every primary teacher's classroom practice. She combines the theory of retrieval practice with what actually happens in the primary classroom providing lots of practical takeaways teachers can use to improve teaching and learning. I thoroughly recommend this book to all primary teachers and those in training.

**Kevin McLaughlin, senior lecturer in ITT (primary).
@_kevinmcl**

Whether or not you are familiar with Kate's work, this is a must read for all primary educators. What really sets this book apart is the way Kate weaves strands of research with powerful examples of practical application in an extremely accessible way. Throw in a stellar supporting cast of fantastic primary practitioners providing a variety of case studies, and what you have is a book that will help all schools strengthen and deepen children's learning.

**Daniel Childs, headteacher at
Ryarsh Primary School. @danielwchilds**

As a primary practitioner and assessment and curriculum leader, Kate's evidenced-informed approach to retrieval has been incredibly influential. The practical – and crucially – teacher friendly suggestions with supportive resources have become an integral part of our lesson design and structure. The school has certainly noticed, through use of pupil voice, children remembering more about what has been taught and being confident to articulate this clearly. If you are involved in developing classroom practice and lesson design, this for me is a must read.

**David Vann, assistant headteacher and
curriculum and assessment lead.**

You will be hard pushed to find someone more knowledgeable about retrieval practice theory and more experienced at translating it into the classroom than Kate Jones. *Retrieval Practice: Primary. A Guide for Primary Teachers and Leaders* provides a powerful synthesis of the underpinning research on retrieval practice and how to apply this in the classroom – the challenge of evidence-informed practice. This book successfully rises to this challenge! Intentionally blending the best available evidence with a deep understanding of the primary context via interviews with a wide range of primary teachers, Kate puts forward actionable strategies and practical techniques that can be applied across the primary curriculum. It is a book that I wish was available when I was teaching in the primary classroom, and I will certainly be drawing upon it to inform the design and delivery of national professional development programmes.

Kathryn Morgan, capacity improvement advisor at the Teaching School Hub Council. @KathrynMorgan_2

Once again, Kate Jones has presented the evidence and activities for the effective delivery of retrieval practice. Upfront, Kate admits that she is not a primary expert but she has clearly put the work in to find out what could work and in doing so shows an acute understanding of what primaries uniquely need. In doing this, she presents the reader with an exceptionally well researched and accessible book for all phases. This is the retrieval book that primary didn't know it wanted but it actually needed and, for me, it's a must read!

Sonia Thompson, Headteacher/Director at St. Matthew's C. E. Primary Research and Support School. @son1bun

Every primary teacher knows the sheer pleasure that pupils take in becoming masters of their favourite topics. From the names of dinosaurs to the parables of the Bible, young children show a remarkable capacity to learn huge amounts. Precisely how to encourage, organise and promote this retrieval is both an art and a science, and Kate Jones's magnificent book guides primary teachers through blending the perfect cocktail of both. With busy teachers in mind, there is unpatronising and clear insights from state-of-the-art research, as well as hard-won professional experience from a range of primary specialists. This is a book that primary teachers will fall in love with, and will supercharge pupil learning for the long term.

Jon Hutchinson, Director of Training and Development at Reach Foundation. @jon_hutchinson_

CONTENTS

FOREWORD
BY CLARE SEALY

There are two equally unhelpful ways in which a primary school might respond to the growing interest in retrieval practice. The first is to reject it as not relevant for primary aged children. The second is to seek to implement it in exactly the same way as it is described in many secondary schools. In this book, Kate helpfully steers a path between these two misguided options and shows how, when thoughtfully implemented and based on research with children at primary age, retrieval practice is a powerful way of strengthening learning. Any staff in primary schools seeking to build or strengthen a culture of retrieval should make sure they have read this book!

While it is true that most of the research on retrieval practice has been carried out on older children and/or away from the classroom, this does not mean there is no evidence of its effectiveness with primary aged children. Kate clearly outlines this research and what it tells us. Retrieval practice *is* effective for this age group, but needs to be done slightly differently from how it is done with secondary aged children.

Whereas older students benefit from free recall tasks, younger primary aged children need an element of guided recall. For example, whereas with older children one might ask, 'Tell me everything you know about sloths', with younger children it would be helpful to give gentle prompts such as 'Tell me what you know about what sloths eat' and then 'Tell me what you know about how sloths move'. Retrieval practice works best when it enables children to be successful.

Chapter 5 on retrieval cues and free recall expands on this key insight. Something that seems blatantly obvious now I've read it but was actually new to me, was advice from McDermott and Roediger that Kate shared, 'The key to good retrieval is developing effective cues, ones that will lead the rememberer back to the encoded information.' As Kate puts it, use the same or similar cues at the encoding and retrieval stages. For example, the same diagram of the water cycle used to explain the concept is used later as a retrieval prompt. The amount of scaffolding can be adjusted. In some cases, the terms for each part of the cycle could be provided with the child only having to remember which term goes where. Or the challenge could be increased by only providing the first letter of each term. Or then again, the diagram could be completely blank.

Cued recall is about providing the smallest hint possible to enable recall. This might be a picture, a mnemonic, or a partially filled in table. In this way retrieval practice can be differentiated, with the amount of missing information varying depending on the learning needs of the child. There is a lot more to retrieval practice than quizzing! Games, verbal recall – with or without a partner – and writing (possibly on a mini white board) are other ways that previous learning can be retrieved and therefore strengthened.

Because multiple choice quizzes rely on recognition memory rather than recall memory, they are sometimes slightly frowned on by retrieval purists as not really providing the most effective context for retrieval practice. However, in the primary school context, where an element of prompting enhances the process, low stakes multiple choice quizzes are really useful. Kate gives us a helpful tour of how to use multiple choice quizzes well, including the importance of writing plausible distractors, ideally using your children's own misconceptions. I particularly liked the suggestion of adding in an extra column where children can, if they wish, elaborate further on an answer. In this way, primary children can be gradually introduced to opportunities for free recall alongside the more scaffolded approach provided by a multiple choice quiz. Free recall should not be banned for this age group, but should be introduced judiciously, by teachers aware of what the research seems to indicate about the usefulness of cued recall for younger children.

As well as opening up the research for us, Kate also shares case studies from primary practitioners. These show us how actual teachers on the ground are putting the research into practice. I particularly enjoyed the case study from Ella Martin of New Horizons Primary School which described how they had worked as a school to embed retrieval practice across the school community. It is one thing to have a good idea, it is another thing entirely to implement it effectively. Ella describes how the school shared the idea not only with staff, but also with children and parents.

There is plenty of practical guidance here for those seeking to introduce or improve how they do retrieval practice. As well as the case studies and various examples of formats to use, the book ends with QR codes linking to a variety of other resources. It is a great resource, and one I wish I had recourse to when I was introducing retrieval practice as a headteacher.

Clare Sealy, head of curriculum and standards, States of Guernsey. Previously Headteacher of St Matthias Primary School, Tower Hamlets. @ClareSealy

INTRODUCTION

Retrieval Practice: Primary. A Guide for Primary Teachers and Leaders has been an absolute joy and privilege to write. As the understanding of retrieval practice is becoming more well-known and widely discussed, teachers are continuing to ask questions and search for answers to further improve their classroom practice. The purpose of this book is to ask questions, investigate, share and reflect on retrieval practice in a primary school context with younger learners.

I cannot guarantee to have all the answers, but I have tried to support primary school leaders, teachers, students and families as best as I can. Many primary school teachers and leaders asked me to write this book, based on my previous books that focus on retrieval practice. I hope I do not disappoint, and I hope I am able to support primary teachers and leaders in their journey to effectively embed retrieval practice across the curriculum.

I have experience working in and with primary schools, but I am a secondary specialist. Writing this book has been a wonderful learning process for me and where there were gaps in my knowledge, experts across the primary sector and academia have very kindly helped me. This support has taken many forms, including conversations, interviews and the featured case studies.

The role of classroom observation has been much more significant while writing this book than in my previous works. I have observed the Early Years Foundation Stage (EYFS) and Year 6, and every year in between. I have watched morning maths, foundation subject lessons, literacy sessions and much more. I have observed children learning, talked to children about their learning, asked lots of questions and had the privilege to teach younger children during this process too (the undeniable highlight for me).

As part of my research, I carried out a series of conversations with primary teachers and leaders. I had discussions online – via Zoom, Teams, and Google Hangouts – telephone calls and some in-person conversations over coffee and cake. The conversations were very informal, with participants being encouraged to feel free to lead the discussion in any direction they wished. For the majority of my conversations, I asked the following questions to gain some insight prior to writing this book.

Q1) Where are you (either as an individual or collectively as a school) in terms of retrieval practice implementation?

Q2) What challenges or barriers have you experienced with retrieval practice in your school or with your class?

Q3) Have staff and/or students noticed any benefits of retrieval practice?

Q4) Have you informed or involved the wider school community (parents, carers and families) with regards to retrieval practice?

Q5) Have you experienced, or do you plan to offer, professional development for staff linked to retrieval practice?

Q6) How can I help you?

These questions can be useful for you to reflect on or discuss with your colleagues. They resulted in fascinating exchanges and naturally led onto other talking points. I noticed patterns emerging; for example, most schools I spoke to felt they had successfully embedded retrieval practice within core subjects but felt more was needed across foundation subjects. Most teachers told me they had received some training or support with retrieval practice but wanted more. Many leaders said they were keen to offer further professional development opportunities linked to retrieval practice in the future.

Every conversation was unique, and helped me shape this book by showing me which areas to focus on; for example, question 4 (about informing and involving parents and carers) inspired me to write chapter 8, focusing on sharing retrieval practice across the wider school community and offering guidance as to how that can be done. Question 6, where I asked how I could help, was also very insightful and again inspired a lot of the content here, as ultimately that is what I hope to do; help others.

I was pleased and impressed to learn what many individual teachers or school communities are already doing with retrieval practice. As a result, I asked them to contribute with case studies so their excellent practice could be shared with readers. These case studies really are brilliant and showcase evidence-informed practice and the benefits of collaboration and continually learning from one another.

There is a large amount of robust research and evidence about retrieval practice but there is a lack of empirical evidence about retrieval practice in a primary school setting. It is clear that more research is needed with a focus on younger children. I believe this will be published in the future as we continue to learn more and ask more questions, and as our knowledge and understanding of memory evolves. There were challenges writing this book, but none that weren't worth taking on.

There will be readers of this book who will have read all my previous books about retrieval practice, or perhaps one or two of them, and there will be others who have not yet read anything I have written. This always brings challenges in terms of knowing where to pitch the content, and of being careful to avoid repetition for returning readers. I have included examples of techniques and resources from my previous books (in addition to lots of new ideas) but if I have covered them in depth before, I have only mentioned or summarised them briefly here.

There are QR codes at the back of the book that direct readers to useful websites, including a page where all my retrieval practice templates, resources and guides can be downloaded freely. Please do use these resources, amend if you wish and feel free to share with others.

I have aimed to combine theory and practice throughout. There will be ideas, resources and strategies that are better suited to different year groups, or work well with some subjects and not others. Whether something is relevant or applicable will be decided by the classroom teacher as they know the context of their classroom. Although nuance and context are key, I believe there are practical takeaways for every primary teacher and every primary classroom.

I hope you find this book interesting, informative and useful. I hope it leads to reflections on your own practice as well as the development of practical techniques you can introduce in your classroom and apply across the curriculum. I hope it encourages more dialogue and conversations between colleagues, teams and schools around retrieval practice and its role within the primary curriculum.

If you would like to discuss the book, share your feedback and reflections or ask any further questions then please don't hesitate to get in touch!

Kate

Twitter – @KateJones_Teach

Instagram – @KateJones_Teach

Facebook – KateJonesTeaching

LinkedIn – https://www.linkedin.com/in/katejoneslovetoteach87/

Contact page via www.lovetoteach87.com

CHAPTER 1
RETRIEVAL PRACTICE: THE RESEARCH

Memory matters …

How would you describe your memory?

I regularly ask adults and children to describe their memory. Ask this question to your friends, colleagues or students and consider their responses. When I ask others how they would describe their memory, many people tell me they have a terrible, poor or patchy memory. The majority of the responses are always negative, but that shows a lack of understanding about and appreciation of memory.

We would be lost and unable to function without our memory. From the moment we wake up in the morning, every step and action we take is driven by memory. The majority of the actions we perform day in and day out are done automatically as part of the daily routines in our lives. We store far more information in our memory than we would ever be able to access at a single given point. The fact that we are not overwhelmed by all the memories we have stored is because of our ability to organise and recall relevant information when needed (although the level of ease and challenge to recall that relevant information varies). Memory is marvellous.

Memory is vital for daily life and life long learning. Professor Michael C. Anderson is an expert in the field of human memory, and has beautifully described how special learning is, 'Learning is miraculous. It transforms babies into college students and college students into Nobel-winning scientists, artists, and even on occasion professors. Learning is after all, the reason why you are reading the very sentence that you are reading at this precise moment.'[1] Learning is miraculous, and memory – among other factors and influences – plays a very significant role in this process. Our memory deserves a lot more credit than we often give it!

---

1   Baddeley, A., Anderson, M. C. and Eysenck, M. (2009). *Memory*. Hove, England: Psychology Press. Page 113.

It is understandable why people – adults and children alike – can be critical of their own memory. It can feel like our memories are letting us down at times, especially when we forget something we feel we should be able to recall! Memory can also lead to people feeling humiliated or embarrassed, for example forgetting the name of someone we have met before or the failure to recall something when we need it. As frustrating as this can be when it occurs, it is a part of life and a part of learning, and this needs to be understood by teachers and students.

Understanding of memory, such as an awareness of the limitations of working memory and harnessing the power of long-term memory, is absolutely essential for any educator. Retrieval practice is the process of recalling learned information from long-term memory, with little or no support. Every time a memory is recalled from long-term memory it is altered and strengthened. Recalling information can be challenging and difficult but it is an effective teaching and learning strategy for students of all ages, and is worth embracing.

Retrieval practice is an evidence-informed strategy which supports and enhances learning and progress. It is not considered an assessment strategy (although during an assessment recall takes place) because it is very much considered formative rather than summative assessment and carried out to support learning, not measure it. Retrieval practice is often associated with revision and preparation for older students as they sit formal examinations, but it is a strategy to be used with all learners of all ages. There is undoubtedly a place for retrieval practice in the primary classroom.

What we ask students to recall, whether it be facts, vocabulary, ideas, concepts, or experiences, is known in cognitive psychology as the target memory (also known as the target trace). If I ask you to recall what you ate for lunch yesterday, that is the target memory. You would recall it and bring it to mind and share it with me (if you can recall it that is, but as I am asking you about yesterday it is highly likely you will be able to recall that target memory). We need to be explicit with students about what the target memories are, especially younger children at primary school because they may recall information that is generalised, vague or irrelevant without realising they are doing so. I will explain later in the book how this can be achieved.

Cognitive psychologists Alan Baddeley, Michael W. Eysenck and Michael C. Anderson write, 'When we search for a target in memory, we usually have some idea of what we are looking for.'[2] As teachers we need to support students to find target memories, and we can do so by carefully considering the questions we ask and the retrieval tasks we design.

Baddeley, Eysenck and Anderson define retrieval as the 'process of recovering a target memory based on one or more cues, subsequently bringing that target into awareness'.[3] Younger learners need cues, guidance and scaffolding to support them with their recall (this is explained more later in the chapter). Chapter 5 explains how teachers can provide effective retrieval cues to support children to retrieve target memories and then gradually remove those cues as knowledge, confidence and retrieval strength increases.

Evidence-informed practice

Senior educational psychologists and authors Jane Yeomans and Christopher Arnold describe cognitive psychology in their book, *Teaching, Learning and Psychology* as the study of mental processes, attempting to describe the mind and how it works.[4] Cognitive psychology is important, but it is only one piece of the wider educational picture. Teachers cannot be expected to have the same level of expertise as specialists in the field of psychology because there is a wide range of other areas teachers and leaders have to be knowledgeable in, such as behaviour, safeguarding, subject knowledge, pedagogical knowledge, knowledge of their students, and much more.

Despite the significance of the role memory plays in education and learning, it is only in recent years that cognitive psychology has become a dominant part of the education discourse. Psychologists Baddeley, Eysenck and Anderson explain that with the study of memory, 'Theories develop and change, and different people will hold different theories to explain the same data.' They further add, 'Fortunately, there is a great deal of general agreement between different groups studying the psychology of memory, even though they tend to use different terminology.'[5]

---

2   Baddeley, A., Anderson, M. C. and Eysenck, M. (2009). *Memory*. Hove, England: Psychology Press. Page 240.

3   Ibid. Page 241.

4   Yeomans, J. and Arnold, C. (2006). *Teaching, Learning and Psychology*. Abingdon: Routledge. Page 58.

5   Baddeley, A., Anderson, M. C. and Eysenck, M. (2009). *Memory*. Hove, England: Psychology Press. Page 5.

I am not a cognitive psychologist, scientist or researcher. I am a classroom teacher, so the perspective of this book is that of a teacher writing for fellow teachers. Applying the research and evidence findings from cognitive psychology in the classroom, and more specifically the primary classroom, is another piece of the picture entirely.

I take great pride in being an evidence-informed teacher, leader and author, but what exactly does evidence-informed mean? As with most terms in education, it is open to interpretation (which is not a bad thing as it can lead to interesting debate and discussion), but I feel it's important to establish a shared understanding of being evidence-informed, as I will refer to this term throughout the book.

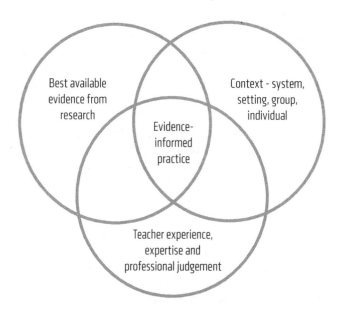

The diagram above is a very clear and useful visual explanation of what it means to be evidence-informed. The diagram was published in *Impact*, the magazine for Chartered College of Teaching (CCT) members, and shows how evidence is only one element of being evidence-informed. It has to be combined with teacher experience, expertise and judgement, and the context must be considered too.

In terms of the best available evidence from the research, it is fair to say there is a robust amount of evidence from research claiming retrieval practice is an effective teaching and learning strategy, both inside and outside of the classroom. I have spent a lot of time reading research and engaging with evidence about retrieval practice, which in itself can be overwhelming due to the sheer volume of content published. There are other challenges involved such as accessibility (although this has improved dramatically in recent years) and gaining clarity, as teachers aren't often the intended audience for published journals or studies relating to human memory.

It is not just the evidence I have engaged with that has led to my enthusiasm and desire to find out more about retrieval practice and share it with others. The evidence is in alignment with my own experiences in the classroom, and through using retrieval practice regularly with my students I was able to observe the many benefits it brings. My students' confidence increased as they were progressing, learning and flourishing, which in turn led to an increase in my confidence as a teacher.

Evidence has informed my practice, but it does not provide all the answers, it never will and nor should it. To rely too heavily on evidence from research would be to disregard the knowledge, experience and expertise that one can only achieve from time spent in the classroom; teaching and interacting with children. It is teachers who must apply the findings of research in order to design questions, create tasks and develop resources to promote retrieval practice in the classroom. Teachers and school leaders have to regularly reflect on their practice and adapt it based on the context and conditions of their classrooms and their learners.

This book aims to be reflective of the diagram from the CCT as I have referenced and drawn on a wide range of research studies and findings in addition to combining my classroom experiences with those of primary teachers and leaders from across the UK and further afield. I reached out to many leading academics to ask questions and find answers or check for accuracy. Research and evidence are embedded throughout this book but this chapter specifically focuses on what research can tell us about retrieval practice in the primary classroom. There are also contributions from other teachers, ranging from anecdotes to reflections and all have their place in this evidence-informed book.

The Education Endowment Foundation (EEF) published a guidance report in December 2019 entitled *Putting evidence to work: A school's guide to implementation*. This guidance report offered useful advice as to how to become evidence-informed through effective implementation. The

EEF is an independent charity that aims 'to support teachers and school leaders to use evidence of what works – and what doesn't – to improve educational outcomes, especially for disadvantaged children and young people'.[6] The guidance reports and toolkits published on their website can be accessed and downloaded freely, and their recommendations are based on a review of research and literature combined with consultations with experts across different fields.

The report warns that, 'In our collective haste to do better for pupils, new ideas are often introduced with too little consideration for how the changes will be managed and what steps are needed to maximise the chances of success. Too often the who, why, where, when, and how are overlooked, meaning implementation risks becoming an "add on" task expected to be tackled on top of the day-to-day work. As a result, projects initiated with the best of intentions can fade away as schools struggle to manage these competing priorities.' Retrieval practice is vulnerable to being misunderstood and mutated through rushed implementation.

The report instructed schools to, 'Treat implementation as a process, not an event; plan and execute in stages.' This advice is certainly applicable to retrieval practice. Time is necessary for any effective implementation and the EEF summary poster advised schools to, 'Allow enough time for effective implementation, particularly in the preparation stage; prioritise appropriately.' Constructive advice that is wholly relevant to the implementation of retrieval practice.

This message from the EEF resonated with me, 'Ultimately, it doesn't matter how great an educational idea or intervention is in principle; what really matters is how it manifests itself in the day-to-day work of people in schools.' This is a message I have tried to stress many times. The evidence from research about retrieval practice as an effective teaching and learning strategy is very positive, but the success of this – or any – strategy will depend on the implementation and application within the classroom.

The learning and remembering process

I regularly reference the work of the late Arthur W. Melton, a leading and highly respected researcher in the field of human memory. The learning process as illustrated by Melton (below) has informed the way I plan and deliver lessons.[7]

---

6   EEF (2022). Homepage. Available at: https://educationendowmentfoundation.org.uk/

7   Melton, A. W. (1963). Implications of short-term memory for a general theory of memory. *Journal of Verbal Learning and Verbal Behavior*, 2, 1–21.

The three main stages of learning and remembering are encoding, storage and retrieval. Although they are all important, significant, interconnected and reliant upon the others, they are not necessarily considered as equals in terms of their value. In an interview conducted in 1991, well known cognitive psychologist Endel Tulving stated that the key process in memory is retrieval. Despite that statement, the two prior phases of encoding and storage must be understood by teachers and considered when planning and teaching.

Two leading experts in the field of retrieval practice are Kathleen B. McDermott and Henry L. Roediger, both currently professors at Washington University in St. Louis. They write, 'Remembering episodes involves three processes: encoding information (perceiving it and relating it to past knowledge), storing it (maintaining it over time), and then retrieving it (accessing the information when needed). Failure can occur at any stage, leading to forgetting or having false memories.'[8]

Yeomans and Arnold refer to encoding as 'the process by which information transfers to memory'[9] and in order for information to be encoded the learner must be paying attention. There has been a lot of enthusiasm with retrieval practice (I am a prime example of that enthusiasm) but the attention and encoding stage cannot be rushed or neglected in the classroom. For information to be recallable it must be encoded and transferred to long-term memory.

When students encounter new information and material, it is stored briefly in what is commonly referred to as working memory. When people speak negatively about their memory it is likely they are unknowingly referring to working memory, which is limited in terms of both capacity and duration; how much information we can hold in it and how long for.

---

8   McDermott, K. B. and Roediger, H. L. (2013). Memory (Encoding, Storage, Retrieval). In R. Biswas-Diener & E. Diener (Eds), Noba textbook series: *Psychology*. Champaign, IL: DEF publishers.

9   Yeomans, J. and Arnold, C. (2006). *Teaching, Learning and Psychology*. Abingdon: Routledge. Page 58.

Peterson and Peterson investigated the duration of working memory and the various factors that cause working memory to decay.[10] They concluded that almost all information stored in working memory and not rehearsed is lost within 18 to 30 seconds. This explains why a person can walk to a room to get something, and when they enter the room they have forgotten what they needed. In a classroom environment a student can be patiently waiting to answer a question with their hand up in the air and by the time the teacher asks for their response they have forgotten what they were going to say! We should use those real life examples and experiences inside and outside of the classroom to explain the limitations of working memory and reassure students.

There is some debate among academics as to how much information can be held at any given time in working memory, but I don't think as teachers we need to fixate on this figure. It's just important to be aware of these limitations and recognise they are universal for all learners, although working memory capacity can vary. Dr Amishi Jha writes that, 'Working memory capacity is really the ability to hold and manipulate information while you're actively trying to block out distraction.'[11] Everyone has and does experience the struggle brought on by working memory limitations.

There are many things we do in our daily lives because we know we can't rely on our working memory to hold certain relevant information. For example, using a bookmark to record what page we have read up to, writing a shopping list so we don't forget items or storing phone numbers in our mobile's contacts so we don't need to recall them from memory. I think it's very important that we explain to students about the limitations of working memory as they may otherwise assume they are stupid or form incorrect beliefs that their memory isn't good.

From EYFS to adults, working memory impacts different areas of teaching and learning. One in ten students has poor working memory that has a negative effect on their learning[12] but it is possible to communicate information and instructions to students in a way that doesn't overload their working memory. This is where knowledge of dual coding and cognitive load theory is relevant and can be helpful.

10   Peterson, L. R. and Peterson, M. J. (1959). Short-term retention of individual verbal items, *Journal of Experimental Psychology*, 58, 193-198.

11   Amishi, J. P. (2021). *Peak Mind: Find your focus, own your attention, invest 12 minutes a day.* London: Piatkus.

12   Gathercole, S. and Alloway, T. (2008). *Working Memory and Learning: A Practical Guide for Teachers.* London: Sage Publications.

Dr Susan E. Gathercole and Dr Tracy Packiam Alloway have written extensively about working memory. If you are interested in learning more about working memory and learning, I have recommended their book at the end of this chapter. Gathercole and Alloway point out that there are many misconceptions held about students with problems linked to working memory. Assumptions can be made that students are lazy or not trying, they may appear disengaged or lacking motivation, and can struggle with attention and focus during lessons. Behaviour problems can be linked to working memory problems but not in all instances.[13]

Poor working memory can impact students' ability to follow instructions or keep up with the pace in the lesson. They might be reluctant to contribute in class and become confused, frustrated or overwhelmed. If any of the above apply to a child in your class, it may be worth discussing or raising concerns about working memory with the school special educational needs co-ordinator (SENDCO) or additional learning needs co-ordinator (ALNCO).

Encoding and retrieval are linked, as it can help learners to encode new information when they can relate it to what they already know, thus establishing and understanding links between new knowledge and prior knowledge. Teachers can take advantage of these connections when planning and designing a curriculum.

Encoding involves the process of recoding; this involves converting the information that is being delivered into something that makes sense to the learner. This is another reason why explicit, clear and thorough explanations are so important. Encoding is selective, as there is often so much happening around us that our memory is selective as to what is or isn't encoded; Pedro De Bruyckere describes it as acting like a spam filter.[14] Therefore we need to repeat points and content that need to be encoded and later recalled as target memories.

McDermott and Roediger refer to storage as, 'The stage in the learning/ memory process that bridges encoding and retrieval; the persistence of memory over time' and they describe retrieval as, 'The process of accessing stored information.'[15] It is the aim of the teacher to support

---

13   Gathercole, S. and Alloway, T. (2008). *Working Memory and Learning: A Practical Guide for Teachers*. London: Sage Publications.

14   De Bruyckere, P. (2018). *The Ingredients for Great Teaching*. London: Sage Publishing.

15   McDermott, K. B. and Roediger, H. L. (2013). Memory (Encoding, Storage, Retrieval). In R. Biswas-Diener & E. Diener (Eds), Noba textbook series: *Psychology*. Champaign, IL: DEF publishers.

students with the transfer of information to long-term memory. Long-term memory is very different to working memory in terms of capacity and duration; at this point the limitations of long-term memory are unknown, simply because it is so powerful!

Vast amounts of information can be stored in long-term memory, but just storing it is not enough. We need students to be able to access and recall information from long-term memory and do so quickly, with ease and accuracy. This is where the process of retrieval practice is essential, as every time already learned material and information is recalled from long-term memory that memory is changed to make it more recallable in the future. There is further discussion of storage and retrieval strength in the next chapter, as this plays a key role in effective curriculum design and development.

Why did Tulving say the key process in memory is retrieval, suggesting it is more important than encoding and storage? The reason for this is that humans encode and store huge amounts, everything that is attended to, but not all of that (or even most of it) is retrieved. There can be unintentional recall where memories are provoked by cues around us, but learning involves the process of actively and deliberately retrieving target memories from long-term memory.

Retrieval practice should not be considered as the final part in the learning process (although this is perhaps implied in the Melton model). I have written previously that we want students to be able to solve problems instead of memorising solutions and be able to make links, connections and provide rich explanations rather than simply repeat or regurgitate facts, numbers, quotes or dates. To think retrieval practice focuses on isolated factual recall is to misunderstand the purpose and power of regular retrieval practice.

Once students have demonstrated they can retrieve information correctly and confidently they need to maintain that ability, to ensure the target memory remains readily accessible as opposed to becoming slower and harder to recall. After successful retrieval, students will also need to apply their knowledge and transfer that knowledge to different contexts or have it accessible to refer to at a later date when making connections between prior learning and new content.

The extended learning and remembering process (Jones, 2022)

The learning and remembering process here is seen as it relates to cognitive psychology; there are of course many other elements that contribute to cognitive, emotional and social development for learners of all ages.

Learning versus performance

Linked to the learning process is a vital distinction that all teachers should be aware of: learning versus performance. This is becoming more well known in education, and if you are familiar with it already please do still read on as I have provided examples to put this distinction into a classroom context. Professors Robert A. Bjork and Elizabeth L. Bjork have written extensively about the distinction between performance and learning. I have been very fortunate to discuss this directly with them both and ask questions about what the implications of it are for teachers and students in the classroom.[16]

Performance demonstrates whether to-be-learned knowledge or skills can be produced during the instruction phase itself, but this is not always a reliable indicator of learning. The Bjorks argue that what teachers can measure during the instruction process, in a lesson, is performance but not (yet) learning. This links with the observation by Paul A. Kirschner, John Sweller and Richard E. Clark that learning occurs when there is a change in long-term memory.[17] Performance can be dependent on cues that are present during the lesson but are unlikely to be present at a later time in a different context, when that same skill or knowledge is required.

Bjork and Bjork write that, 'We can be misled by our current performance. Conditions of learning that make performance improve rapidly often fail to support long-term retention and transfer, whereas conditions that create challenges and slow the rate of apparent learning

16   Jones, K. (2021). Meet the Bjorks: The research legacy teachers must know. *TES*. 27 July 2021. Available at: https://www.tes.com/magazine/teaching-learning/general/meet-bjorks-research-legacy-teachers-must-know

17   Kirschner, P., Clark, R. and Sweller, J. (2006). Why Minimal Guidance During Instruction Does Not Work : An Analysis of the Failure of Constructivist , Discovery , Problem-Based , Experiential , and Inquiry-Based Teaching. *Educational Psychologist*, 41. 75-86.

often optimize long-term retention and transfer.'[18] To simplify, we can consider checking for understanding as performance, and using retrieval practice as checking for long-term learning.

An example of measuring or assessing performance and later focusing on learning can be with the use of 'exit tickets'. This simple technique has existed for a long time in the classroom, previously it was often used as the plenary to check for learning but now our understanding of learning has developed and changed, the purpose of the exit ticket must change too. Exit tickets tend to consist of three to five questions (or problems) that students answer at the end of a lesson. Exit tickets should be short, clear and concise (multiple choice and short answer questions are ideal). The intention is to home in on and assess understanding of the main points of the lesson; the essential elements and what will later become the target memories. If the information isn't required to be recalled in the future or doesn't support understanding it shouldn't be included on an exit ticket.

The teacher can collect the exit tickets quickly and easily to skim and scan and check; they can provide useful data and insight for teachers in terms of checking for understanding, and lead to responsive teaching. At this point in the lesson and learning process, performance is being reviewed as not enough time has passed to check for long-term learning and recall. I would add that checking for understanding should be a constant feature within a lesson and not just at the end with an exit ticket, so an exit ticket is simply one way of checking for understanding.

Using exit tickets at the end of a lesson helps to check for understanding as misconceptions and misunderstandings can be highlighted. This can inform and guide future planning for the teacher, allowing them to see whether to move on or revisit content from the lesson if needed. This is helpful as a method of formative assessment but is not to be confused with long-term learning. Exit tickets at the end of a lesson cannot tell or show teachers if information has been transferred to, and can be recalled from, long-term memory. To do that it is necessary to revisit the questions or problems at a later date to find out what students can or cannot recall. Despite this limitation there is a way exit tickets can be used for

18   Bjork, E. L. and Bjork, R. A. (2011). Making things hard on yourself, but in a good way: Creating desirable difficulties to enhance learning. In M. A. Gernsbacher, R. W. Pew, L. M. Hough, J. R. Pomerantz (Eds.) & FABBS Foundation, *Psychology and the real world: Essays illustrating fundamental contributions to society* (56–64). New York: Worth Publishers.

both checking for understanding and long-term learning. A strategy I have carried out with my classes is to recycle a previously used exit ticket into an entrance ticket, ideal for a 'do now' task at the start of a lesson to focus on retrieval practice. The same questions and problems can be posed (or adapted) for students to answer from memory.

Students have commented on this or asked why they are answering the same set of questions, but at this point I talk to them about the distinction between performance and learning. The entrance ticket allows students the opportunity to recall information from prior lessons, with the questions from the original exit ticket being used to assess long-term learning. When we ask students questions is key; the timing of questions and tasks will determine the focus on performance or learning.

The example below shows the same template and the same questions to be distributed to students, the key difference being the timing of the exit ticket – a performance task – versus the entrance ticket which is essentially a learning task. Doing this also illustrates to students the importance of the lesson content and how it shouldn't be forgotten once the lesson is over. Exit often implies the end of a process or journey but an exit ticket is used in the early stages of the learning process when checking performance, understanding and comprehension.

Exit Ticket

Q1. What does the term 'heir' mean?

Q2. Why was there confusion about who should be King in 1066?

Q3. Who were the three main contenders to the throne in 1066?

Entrance Ticket

Q1. What does the term 'heir' mean?

Q2. Why was there confusion about who should be King in 1066?

Q3. Who were the three main contenders to the throne in 1066?

I have kept exit tickets and asked students to compare and contrast their responses from the exit and entrance tickets. This was interesting as some of the answers differed in terms of accuracy and depth. Some students were able to improve their answers whereas other students struggled when recalling the answers from long-term memory. This demonstrates the impact of forgetting on learning. An additional benefit of using exit tickets as entrance tickets is the workload implication for teachers repurposing a resource with their classes; this is a good move, not a lazy one.

Most classroom tasks can either be used or adapted to suit the purpose of measuring performance or learning. I have used the task 'keyword spotlight' with different classes and ages, the focus is the keyword under the spotlight, in this example it is 'democracy'. During a lesson discussing and exploring democracy I can ask students to complete this task. All of the information required will have been discussed in the lesson and fresh in students' minds. This is at the point of attention and encoding and is checking for student understanding.

In your own words write a definition:	Use the term correctly in a sentence:	Create a question where the keyword is the answer:
Democracy: A system with a government chosen by the people for the people fairly.	Countries that have a democracy include Britain, USA and Australia.	What is the system where a government is chosen by the people?

Keyword: Democracy

What other words are connected to the keyword?
Election, equality, politics, democrat, political parties, government

Draw a or find a picture to illustrate this keyword:

VOTES

SELF ASSESS YOUR UNDERSTANDING OF THIS KEYWORD: GOT IT!   ALMOST!   NOT YET!

Alternatively, I could wait and ask students to complete this from memory at a later date. No notes or support but instead as a retrieval task to find out what students can or cannot recall from long-term memory. This demonstrates the importance of teachers being aware of the different stages of the learning process and the distinction between performance and learning. When the task is carried out with a class will depend on the required purpose and it shows how most tasks can be completed at the encoding stage and then again later on, recycling resources to assess performance and learning.

A final example to illustrate this point about performance versus learning focuses on when to check if learning intentions have been achieved. Learning intentions, also referred to as lesson objectives or big questions, provide a clear focus on the content being covered in a lesson, but learning intentions must be long-term. Learning intentions need to be revisited after time has passed to ensure learning has taken place. Content can be covered within a lesson but as we know, learning happens over time, so it is essential to continually revisit learning intentions at a later date with recall of target memories linked to the intention.

If an observer is in a lesson and wants to find out about the students' learning, they should be present for a retrieval task or ask questions about their prior learning. Even better would be for the observer to return to the same class at a later date and ask questions about the previously taught content to find out what students can recall.

Different types of memory

The term memory is all encompassing and should be considered as an umbrella term because it comprises many different components and functions. Memory is not a single store.

Primary school is a very special and important time in a child's development, learning and progress. The definition of learning by Kirschner, Sweller and Clark describing it as a change in long-term memory and capability is useful, but specifically focuses on learning and is not in reference to a wider holistic education. Many elements and experiences contribute to the school life of a learner, from concerts to field trips and sports day and other memorable events and occasions. For this reason, it is important that all primary teachers are aware of the differences between episodic and semantic memories.

Psychologist and cognitive neuroscientist Endel Tulving is credited for defining the distinction between episodic and semantic memories.

Semantic memory refers to knowledge of the world although it goes beyond simply knowing key facts. For example, knowing the word 'apple' and also knowing the significance of the apple to Adam and Eve, and Isaac Newton, and also knowing what an apple looks and tastes like! When planning, teaching and delivering a knowledge rich curriculum, semantic memory is key.

Episodic memories refer to the capacity to remember specific life events that tend to be connected with powerful emotions. Tulving limited the use of the term 'episodic memory' to situations in which you actually re-experience some aspect of the original episode, for example, remembering a specific feeling from the time. Tulving referred to this as mental time travel. A strong episodic memory can enable us to remember variables such as where we were, what we were doing, how we were feeling and/or who we were with. Most people will have episodic memories from their days at school.

Semantic and episodic memories differ but memories can be both at the same time. Clare Sealy has explained why knowledge of these types of memories is relevant to teachers. She writes on her blog, 'The key purpose of education is to build strong semantic memory, to pass on knowledge built up over centuries to the next generation,' adding, 'If we treat our children with kindness and respect they will have episodic memories of what it was like to be treated kindly and respectfully, which makes it more likely they too will treat others with kindness and respect.'[19] There is a place for both in school but teachers should prioritise semantic memory when focusing on teaching and learning.

Procedural memory is the ability to recall how to do something. Children develop procedural memories from a very young age including learning to walk, talk and then later reading and writing. As children progress, they continue to develop more procedural memories, which is possible because most procedural memories reach the stage of automaticity. Automaticity involves knowing how to do something so well that there is no need to stop and consider each stage of the process, it just happens seamlessly and effortlessly (also known as implicit memory).

A driver will at one point be a novice when they are a learner, but then through lessons and practise they will become an able driver who

---

19   Sealy, C. (2017). Memory not memories - teaching for long term learning. *Primarytim-erydotcom*. Available at: https://primarytimery.com/2017/09/16/memory-not-memo-ries-teaching-for-long-term-learning/

doesn't have to consider every step in the process of driving. Driving simply happens, often referred to as being on auto-pilot. Procedural memory is important in the classroom because once students are familiar with specific activities or skills, the process becomes automatic, therefore working memory is freed up and can instead be used to focus on the content or questions instead of how to complete a task.

Declarative memory contrasts with implicit/procedural memory, as conscious effort is required to recall information from long-term memory. This explicit memory is linked to the recall of semantic or episodic memories. When time and effort is invested to recall target memories, whether that be key facts or in-depth knowledge, this is declarative memory.

Research about retrieval practice with primary school students

The amount of published research and evidence about retrieval practice is overwhelming. However, it has been noted and observed by many that a large amount of this data is a result of research and studies carried out in laboratory conditions, not a school setting. Another issue is that the studies have tended to focus more on secondary and young adult learners, in contrast to younger children in a primary setting. There is evidence from classrooms and there is research focusing on younger children in a primary context but there is a need for more to be done. I have included a variety of sources in this section but as there was a lot to cover, I have aimed to summarise the key findings and evidence I believe will either demonstrate retrieval practice is effective in the primary classroom or offers useful guidance and advice for primary teachers and school leaders.

Research and evidence from laboratory studies can provide useful information and insight for teachers and we should not be dismissive of this but instead recognise both its values and limitations. There is a shift towards more research and studies being carried out in classrooms, but this does come with many challenges. Every classroom is unique, which is wonderful and to be celebrated, but this does result in a large number of variables that have an impact on research, unlike controlled conditions in a laboratory. The majority of the research linked to retrieval practice is carried out in the US, so for reference and context, when referring to research conducted in the US; ages three to five is classified as pre-school, ages five to six is kindergarten and elementary school is ages six to eleven.

A team of well known academics in the field of memory and learning authored a paper in 2016 entitled *Retrieval-Based Learning: Positive Effects of Retrieval Practice in Elementary School Children*. The authors are Jeffrey D. Karpicke, Janell R. Blunt, Megan A. Sumeracki and Stephanie S. Karpicke. They noted that, 'A lot of research has demonstrated that practising retrieval is a powerful way to enhance learning. However, nearly all prior research has examined retrieval practice with college students. Little is known about retrieval practice in children, and even less is known about possible individual differences in retrieval practice.'[20]

The researchers conducted a study with three experiments involving elementary school children aged between nine and eleven years. All took place in classroom conditions during lesson sessions and involved educational content and curriculum materials. The authors noted that, 'Grades 3–5 represent a critical time in children's educational development, because by these grade levels children have learned to read, and they are now increasingly "reading to learn". That is, late elementary school children are beginning to read material and implement strategies on their own in order to learn from what they are reading. Thus it is essential to examine retrieval practice in elementary school children.'[21]

The first experiment focused on finding out if retrieval-based learning strategies – those that had shown to be effective when used by older college students – would result in similar impact and findings with elementary school aged children. The experiment was carried out with 94 children but due to child absences across the four-week period, only 54 students completed all four conditions. I have included this as an example of a variable that can have an impact on research, but it is a challenge and reality of a classroom, trying to support learners that have been absent, and the global pandemic since 2020 has heightened this even further.

The experimental sessions were carried out in classes but the children worked independently. They had to read educational texts from the subject of science and then engage in different learning tasks. These involved creating a concept map with the information presented in front of them, creating a concept map from memory using free recall

---

20   Karpicke, J., Blunt, J., Sumeracki, M. and Karpicke, S. (2016). Retrieval-Based Learn- ing: Positive Effects of Retrieval Practice in Elementary School Children. *Frontiers in Psychology*. 7 (104).

21   Ibid.

(retrieval practice without support or cues), rereading the text and attempting to recall after a second attempt, and cued recall where students were given sentence starters in the second recall period.

The results of the experiment showed that free recall tasks were 'not feasible for promoting learning of educational texts with elementary school children'. It is perhaps not surprising that younger children need more explicit guidance, cues and scaffolding for the initial retrieval task. This is where teacher knowledge of the children in their classes becomes relevant and significant, enabling them to know when to provide retrieval support and how to do so, and then later when to remove that support. These results correlate with my classroom experience of teaching younger students that have struggled with initial free recall tasks and required retrieval cues, which I later removed.

The second experiment focused on the use of concept mapping as a retrieval-based learning activity. A concept map allows the teacher (or researcher in this case) to control and alter the amount of support provided, a concept which is explored more fully in chapter 5. Of the 103 children participating in the second experiment, 79 completed all four conditions, again due to factors such as absences. The authors observed that in this experiment the results were promising, and the children were more successful than in the prior experiment. The authors commented, 'The results of Experiment 2 suggested that concept mapping could serve as an effective retrieval activity with children because the activity affords the opportunity to provide retrieval support.'

Experiment three had a cohort of 89 children, with data based on 85 students once again due to absences. Guided retrieval practice was compared against restudy of educational materials. The findings stated that 'Experiment 3 demonstrated the efficacy of a guided retrieval procedure', adding, 'The results also suggest that, under certain conditions, free recall of educational texts is indeed a feasible task for young children when appropriate scaffolds are put in place to guide and support children's successful recall.'

This publication has been a significant influence and inspiration for the contents of this book. The following chapters act on its evidence with advice, guidance and practical examples for the primary classroom to ensure retrieval practice and the use of retrieval cues support children with their long-term learning. The evidence also highlighted a clear distinction between strategies that work with older students and those which work well with younger learners. There is a danger with trying to force evidence-informed ideas into another context where it may not be transferable, appropriate or effective. Context is key.

One of the authors of this paper and founder of the *Learning Scientists*, Megan Sumeracki, has observed that, 'It seems that in order for retrieval practice to work well with students of any age, we need to ensure that students are successful in the recall activity.'[22] This is a key theme throughout this book; how to provide a desirable level of difficulty and strike a balance between retrieval challenge and retrieval success for students.

Sumeracki further adds, 'Retrieval practice works well for students of many ages and abilities but, for some students, writing out everything they know on a blank sheet of paper may be a daunting task that does not lead to much successful retrieval. To increase success, teachers can implement scaffolded retrieval tasks ... with scaffolding, the students can successfully produce the information and work their way up to recalling the information on their own.'[23] The main headline I took away from reading this paper is that there is a need for guided retrieval practice in the primary classroom.

A study published in 2015, *Test-enhanced learning in third-grade children* by Antonio Jaegera, Raquel Eloísa Eisenkraemerb and Lilian Milnitsky Stein, also highlighted that retrieval practice, with cues, can support learning with younger students. The abstract states:

> *Several recent studies have shown that retrieval is more efficient than restudy in enhancing the long-term retention of memories. However, studies investigating this effect in children are still rare. Here, we report an experiment in which third-grade children initially read a brief encyclopaedic text twice and then either performed a cued recall test on selected target contents of the text or reread the same text twice. A final four-choice memory test about the text's contents was administered to all children after seven days as well as tests measuring their IQ and reading skills. In the final four-choice memory test, children who took the initial cued recall test showed significantly greater performance in comparison with children who restudied the text twice (their responses were 87 and 53% correct, respectively). The results suggest that cued recall tests can elicit very robust testing*

---

22 Sumeracki, M. (ND). How to create retrieval practice activities for elementary students. *The Learning Scientists*. Available at: https://www.learningscientists.org/blog/2017/4/6-1

23 Ibid.

effects in young children, even when complex, educationally relevant materials are used as stimuli.[24]

This is very reassuring and once again illustrates that younger children can also experience the benefits of retrieval-based learning.

Professors Pooja K. Agarwal and Lisa K. Fazio noted that the evidence linked to retrieval practice for learning in a primary context is very positive. They write, 'Based on emerging literature for preschool and elementary school students, there is clear evidence that retrieval practice improves learning in children, starting in infancy.'[25] This message is echoed in much of the literature I have read.

Agarwal and Fazio offer similar advice to that of Sumeracki about providing younger students with scaffolding and support. They advise, 'Provide scaffolding to help young children remember information during retrieval practice. When children do not benefit from retrieval-based learning, it is often because they were unable to retrieve any of the relevant information. By scaffolding their recall, teachers can help students to recall more information. For example, instead of asking broad questions like, "What do you remember about sloths?", teachers can provide additional prompts (e.g., "What do you remember about how sloths move?" or "What do you remember about what sloths eat?").'

They go on to add that, 'The key is to make retrieval practice challenging, but successful. In addition, providing feedback (whether formal or informal) is a great way to ensure that all children, not just those who were able to retrieve the correct information, benefit from retrieval practice. Overall, retrieval practice is an effective way to boost learning for students of all ages.' Agarwal and Fazio have created a free downloadable guide entitled *How to Implement Retrieval-based Learning in Early Childhood Education.* There is a QR code at the back of this book that will direct you to the guide or it can be accessed at https://www.retrievalpractice.org/library.

Chie Hottaa, Hidetsugu Tajikab and Ewald Neumannc authored the 2016 paper *Effects of repeated retrieval on long-term retention in a nonverbal learning task in younger children.* They carried out an experiment with 60

24   Antonio Jaeger, A., Raquel Eloísa Eisenkraemer, R. E. and Stein, L. M. (2015). Test-enhanced learning in third-grade children. *Educational Psychology*, 35:4, 513-521.

25   Fazio, L. K. and Agarwal, P. K. (2020). How to implement retrieval-based learning in early childhood education. *Retrievalpractice.org* Available at: http://pdf.retrievalpractice.org/EarlyChildhoodGuide.pdf

preschool children (aged five to six years) performing a spatial location memory task. The authors outlined that the study was designed to examine whether repeated retrieval improves the retention of location memory for small toys in preschool children.

The researchers were able to demonstrate that the children in the retrieval condition retained location memory for the toys in the experiment longer than those in the study condition. The paper stated, 'The results indicated that retrieval during studying was more beneficial than repeated study for the long-term retention of nonverbal materials for preschool children.' The authors added, 'The current study suggests that repeated retrieval can be an effective strategy for preschool children.'[26]

The findings from another experiment, comparing different methods to support students with spelling, demonstrated that retrieval practice is a useful method to improve accurate recall of spellings. The paper *Beyond the Rainbow: Retrieval Practice Leads to Better Spelling than does Rainbow Writing* published by Professor John Dunlosky and his colleagues compared two common methods of spelling instruction. The conclusion drawn from the results was clear; retrieval practice was a more useful and engaging training method to lead to better spelling.[27]

For any readers unfamiliar with the 'rainbow writing' approach to spelling, it is a popular strategy of repeatedly copying out words in different colours to create a rainbow effect, for example writing out a word in red then writing over that word in orange and so on. The rainbow strategy can appear on the surface to be a useful task, with repetition of spellings being practised, but similar to other ineffective strategies such as re-reading and highlighting it can provide an illusion of learning and a false sense of confidence in contrast to using retrieval techniques.

There is further exploration at the end of this chapter on recent research focusing on retrieval practice, where I have analysed it through a primary lens.

---

26   Hotta, C., Tajika, H. and Neumann, E. (2017). Effects of repeated retrieval on long-term retention in a nonverbal learning task in younger children. *European Journal of Developmental Psychology*, 14:5, 533–544.

27   Jones, A. C., Wardlow, L., Pan, S. C., Zepeda, C., Heyman, G. D., Dunlosky, J., and Rickard, T. C. (2016). Beyond the rainbow: Retrieval practice leads to better spelling than does rainbow writing. *Educational Psychology Review*, 28(2), 385–400.

Spaced practice

I have always considered retrieval practice to go hand in hand with spaced practice (also known as distributed practice or the spacing effect). Asking students questions isn't always retrieval practice, as we have observed with performance versus learning. Asking students to find the answers to questions or search for information from a textbook, class notes or online isn't retrieval practice. Asking students questions in class based on recent explanations or discussion isn't retrieval practice but it can serve other useful purposes such as checking for understanding or consolidation. Asking students to recall target memories is retrieval practice because of the forgetting that has occurred with the passage of time, and this is a key component of both retrieval and spaced practice.

Why isn't spaced practice more widely used or embraced? This question can be answered by both evidence from research studies and experiences from students and teachers. Firstly, spaced practice and spreading out content over time is counter-intuitive, meaning that for teachers and students it makes sense to teach and study content neatly in blocked sections as this is smoother, seems less messy and complicated, and just feels right, as is the case with many popular but ineffective strategies such as re-reading and highlighting. In a primary context it is important not to confuse learners, but it is possible to plan spaced retrieval practice across the primary curriculum.

The Early Career Framework (ECF) in England now places emphasis on memory and cognitive science principles but it is fair to say this has previously been absent from teacher training and education. Many teachers (myself included) were not equipped with the knowledge, understanding and skills to design, develop and deliver a curriculum that promoted spaced practice. Another reason it is not more widely used, I would argue, is the lack of awareness about the distinction between learning versus performance, where teachers taught content and regularly checked for understanding, confusing practice for learning. Spaced retrieval practice should be thought about and considered when planning, designing and delivering a primary curriculum, which is discussed in the next chapter.

At secondary school students are encouraged to space out their independent study but this is not easy and although not impossible, it is not entirely age appropriate at primary school level. Spaced practice requires commitment and organisation. A knowledge organiser can be used to revisit and quiz previously studied content, but younger students require a lot of support, guidance and instruction.

Jon Hutchinson is a primary teacher and director of training and development at the Reach Foundation. During the time I have followed his blogs and Twitter account (@jon_hutchinson_) he has taught me a lot about retrieval practice in a primary setting. The main example of this was a video he created and very generously shared freely on YouTube. In this video Jon explained how the Leitner System works. This is a method of promoting spaced retrieval practice using flashcards that Jon used with his Year 4 class.

I was so impressed by his explanation that I shared it with colleagues, students and parents and carers. Jon explains how flashcards can be created based on the contents of the knowledge organiser and then be used for regular retrieval practice. Many aspects of retrieval practice and spaced practice that I previously believed weren't relevant or possible in a primary context, have been shown by Jon to be extremely useful.

The video by Jon was aimed at parents and carers because if younger children are expected to be using spaced retrieval practice outside of school, they will require support. If you haven't watched the video then I suggest you do so and like I did, share it widely. The QR code at the back of this book that will take you directly to it.

What does the latest research tell us about retrieval practice?

It is clear that the research findings from cognitive science and psychology have shaped government policy across the UK and further afield. The 2019 Ofsted *Education Inspection Framework* stated, 'We can draw on a growing evidence base from the "learning sciences". Learning sciences is a relatively new interdisciplinary field that seeks to apply understanding generated by cognitive science to classroom practice.'[28] The *Early Career Framework* in England (published in 2019) was also influenced by findings from cognitive science, emphasising the importance of teachers new to the profession having an awareness and knowledge of working and long-term memory. As we know in education, policy often shapes practice in the classroom.

2021 was a slightly controversial year for cognitive science, with some clickbait headlines in educational magazines (that didn't often reflect

---

28 Ofsted (2019). *Education inspection framework – overview of research*. London: Ofsted. Available at: https://assets.publishing.service.gov.uk/government/uploads/system/ uploads/attachment_data/file/963625/Research_for_EIF_framework_updated_refer- ences_22_Feb_2021.pdf

the content of the articles let alone the content of the publications) and some educators were questioning the effectiveness of (and the hype around) evidence-informed strategies such as cognitive load theory, dual coding and interleaving.

A potential issue when reports and research findings use the umbrella term 'cognitive science' is that all those strategies can become blurred, which leads to misunderstandings, and research findings become mutated, with false myths and information spreading easily and quickly. This was quite alarming to witness on social media and although I do believe we should be rigorous and ask probing questions about research and evidence findings, it is important not to be motivated and driven by ideology, which was happening and causing division in the profession. Teachers have shared goals; to help our students flourish, progress and learn. However, there are often differences as to how those things can be achieved, but despite this, as a profession we have more that unites us than divides us, or at least we should.

The 2021 EEF review *Cognitive Science approaches in the classroom: A review of the evidence* was conducted by a team consisting of Dr Thomas Perry, Dr Rosanna Lea, Clara Rübner Jørgensen (University of Birmingham), Prof. Philippa Cordingley (CUREE), Prof. Kimron Shapiro, and Prof. Deborah Youdell (University of Birmingham). Additional support was provided and the summary was written by Jonathan Kay and Harry Madgwick of the EEF.

The full report[29] and the summary[30] can be accessed online; the summary consists of 51 pages in contrast to the full report at 372 pages. The report focuses on different aspects of cognitive science and how they might be applied in the classroom. Although the studies were conducted by both teachers and researchers, they were all carried out in classrooms, not laboratories. The aspects covered were: spaced learning, interleaving, retrieval practice, managing cognitive load, working with schemas and multimedia learning (including dual coding).

The key points to consider, as pointed out by the report (with a focus on retrieval practice) are:

---

29   Perry, T., Lea, R., Jørgensen, C. R., Cordingley, P., Shapiro, K., and Youdell, D. (2021). *Cognitive Science in the Classroom.* London: Education Endowment Foundation (EEF) Available at: https://d2tic4wvo1iusb.cloudfront.net/documents/guidance/Cognitive_Science_in_the_classroom_-_Evidence_and_practice_review.pdf?v=1629124467
30   Ibid.

Short, low-stakes tests or 'quizzes' in various formats can be a cheap, easy-to-implement way of recapping material that might strengthen pupils' long-term ability to remember key concepts or information.

Planning test difficulty is particularly important – pupils should be able to retrieve at least some of the content they are tested on.

Quizzing or low-stakes testing may also reveal misconceptions. How will you ensure that where these emerge pupils are supported to overcome them?'

Most, if not all teachers and leaders will be aware that retrieval practice is a low effort and lost cost strategy that can be easily implemented to support learning. These are arguably not new points and suggestions, and it can be disappointing when research reviews don't appear on the surface to share any new insight. But instead we should view this as a positive as it is confirming or supporting current practice in the classroom.

Planning test difficulty links in with the published work of the Bjorks, who have written extensively about 'desirable difficulty'. This term refers to the level of difficulty teachers should provide their students. A desirable difficulty is a level of difficulty that poses challenges for learners, but those challenges can be overcome by a student, given that student's current knowledge and their invested effort.

Robert Bjork uses a video-gaming analogy to illustrate that students can embrace, not avoid, difficulties when they feel they can overcome those difficulties. Level 1 in most video games begins as quite easy, providing the gamer with a taste of success and a boost of motivation to keep going, but the levels will gradually increase in difficulty. The increased challenge is a good example of a desirable difficulty as it can be achieved through increased effort and determination. If the challenge did not increase, it would be too easy and become pointless. If the challenge becomes too tough, it can be demoralising, leading the gamer to abandon the game.

The results of the EEF report are positive and encouraging: teachers should continue with the act of retrieval in lessons. As stated in the report one of the weaknesses of the evidence is that many of the approaches were designed and delivered by researchers rather than classroom teachers. The report notes:

There are examples of teacher-delivered quizzing having a positive impact but given the lack of studies, a firm conclusion is not possible. There are also questions about whether retrieval practice is as effective for more complex or subtle learning beyond rote factual recall. Despite these limitations, the positive impact of the retrieval studies, the good theoretical grounding of the practice, and the low cost of implementing low stakes testing and quizzing generally mean that it is a promising approach that teachers should consider.

At present, the evidence is uncertain about which activity formats are most effective and whether retrieval practice can help students learn 'higher order' or more subtle learning content beyond factual recall. There are, however, a number of factors that teachers should consider when implementing retrieval practice – particularly around whether additional support is required for pupils that struggle. When one provides a test to a group of students, they will – to varying proportions: successfully retrieve some answers; be unable to retrieve others; and erroneously retrieve some answers (for example, misconceptions).

Although a clear effort was made for a spread across age groups this report demonstrated there is a need for further research to be carried out in primary schools and across a wider and diverse range of subjects. 'Studies looked at a wide range of subjects including language, history, maths, science, and English' and 'The studies spanned students from early years to older pupils aged 16–17. There was a good spread across primary and secondary pupils'. Although an absence of evidence from subjects and year groups is disappointing, an absence or lack of evidence does not mean retrieval practice is ineffective and can't be applied effectively. A key theme that emerged from the report was that of nuance, and once a strong grasp of retrieval practice has been achieved this is the next step by focusing on what effective implementation of retrieval practice looks like in our classrooms.

It is worth adding that the EEF have published a range of guidance reports that are specific to primary including the following:

Improving literacy in Key Stage 2. (Second Edition Published 26 November, 2021)

Improving literacy in Key Stage 1. (Second Edition Published 4 September, 2020)

Preparing for Literacy. Seven recommendations to support early language and literacy. (Published 15 June, 2018)

Improving Mathematics in the Early Years and Key Stage 1. (Published 24 January, 2020)

Improving Mathematics in the Early Years and Key Stages 2 and 3. (Published 3 November, 2017)

There are other guidance reports that are applicable and aimed at both primary and secondary.

Also in 2021, Professor Pooja K. Agarwal published a review article with her colleagues, Ludmila D. Nunes and Janell R. Blunt entitled *Retrieval practice consistently benefits student learning: a systematic review of applied research in schools and classrooms.* This review focused solely on retrieval practice and began in January 2018, with a considerable amount of time and research invested into it by leading experts in the field.

Agarwal, Nunes and Blunt analysed nearly 2,000 research abstracts and 50 classroom experiments that met specific criteria set to clearly 'establish a clearer picture of the benefits from retrieval practice in real world educational settings'. This was a turning point as there was a clear emphasis on classroom studies and application, not on laboratory work. In terms of the review the authors explained they had three key aims:

1. To focus on evidence from experiments carried out in a classroom context only (not comparable laboratory studies). This showed that a clear focus was on the application of retrieval practice in a real life setting and learning environment.

2. To inform future directions for research on retrieval practice. As well as providing information, data and answers, research can also result in further questions and areas that need to be addressed and investigated in the future.

3. To clarify recommendations for classroom implementation of retrieval practice. The aim here is to further support teachers and students with the use of retrieval practice to support learning in a school environment.

It is important to establish in this context what the review means when referring to classroom research. The authors stated the following guidelines applied:

Relevant course materials – Information to be learned for research purposes was the same as, or directly related to, assigned course materials.

Individual, not collaborative – All students engaged in retrieval practice individually under the supervision of researchers and instructors.

Closed-book, not open-book - All retrieval practice took place without the use of notes, external learning aids, or the internet.

The review investigated unresolved questions that are often asked and associated with retrieval practice, including:

Is there an optimal frequency of retrieval practice to improve student learning? The answer to this is that there are simply too many variables for us to state a specific amount of time, although there can be optimum timings. The variables include the complexity of the topic, how it links to prior learning, and how often the subject is taught. The review recommends 'educators provide students with opportunities for retrieval practice regardless of the precise timing'. This means that retrieval practice should be a regular classroom routine, but teachers should not fixate on specific timings in terms of the spacing delay and how much time to dedicate within a lesson to the act of retrieval and when to provide feedback. The best guidance for this will come from the professional judgement of the individual teacher.

Do all subjects and age ranges benefit from retrieval practice? In terms of content and subject, most experiments were conducted in science and psychology, with a few in history, spelling and vocabulary, and statistics. The results (similar to the findings from the recent EEF cognitive science report discussed above) demonstrate the need for more applied research across a wider range of subjects. Despite this the authors encourage teachers of all subjects and all ages to use retrieval practice.

Is there a specific type of retrieval practice that is more beneficial than others? The review recommends teachers and students should use both multiple-choice (cued recall) and short answer formats (free recall) for retrieval practice. I was very pleased to read this as it replicates previous advice I have read. I often advise teachers not to rely solely on multiple-choice or free recall as there are benefits and limitations to both approaches. The review encouraged further research on retrieval practice and transfer in applied settings which I and many others hope to see in the near future. All of the different types of retrieval practice are explored and discussed in this book.

The review findings stated the majority of effect sizes indicated medium or large benefits from retrieval practice, saying that, 'for almost all studies reviewed, possible values for effect sizes are in a positive direction, indicating a consistent benefit from retrieval practice on student learning.' Experiments were distributed across education levels and ages, with effect sizes being the largest for studies conducted in middle school classrooms. Although there was a distribution across ages, out of a total of 50 experiments only five focused on elementary school learners but this was recognised by the authors as they encouraged further research for this age group.

In March 2021 Professors Gregory M. Donoghue and John Hattie published *A Meta-Analysis of Ten Learning Techniques*. The purpose of the meta-analysis was to review the ten learning techniques previously identified and reviewed by John Dunlosky and his colleagues in 2013. Dunlosky concluded that retrieval practice and spaced practice are very effective under a wide array of situations, and encouraged teachers and students to use them. Other learning strategies were also reviewed and categorised in terms of their effectiveness in enhancing and improving learning.

Interleaving, self-explanation and elaboration were described as 'promising but more research needed'. Highlighting and underlining were described as not particularly helpful but can be used as a first step toward further study. Rereading was described as having potential to be helpful, but time could be spent using a better strategy, and keyword mnemonics were described as somewhat helpful for learning languages, but the benefits were short lived.

Dunlosky made a clear distinction between practice testing (retrieval practice) and high stakes assessment. The effect of practice testing was considered strong regardless of the test form and effective for students of all ages. The work of Donoghue and Hattie concluded that their meta-analysis is a confirmation of the major findings published by Dunlosky and his colleagues in 2013, therefore confirming the effectiveness of retrieval practice and spaced practice as learning techniques.

The evidence from research is very positive about the use and need for retrieval practice in the primary classroom. It can be frustrating when the focus of research tends to be on specific subjects or age groups more than others, but we should be hopeful and optimistic about further studies that are being conducted or will be conducted in the future. Through reflecting and sharing classroom experiences and combining that with the evidence presented as a profession collectively and collaboratively, we can have a better understanding of what effective retrieval practice looks like in the primary classroom.

Further recommended reading

Working Memory and Learning: A Practical Guide for Teachers. Susan Gathercole and Tracy Packiam Alloway. (2008)

Powerful Teaching: Unleash the Science of Learning. Pooja K. Agarwal and Patrice Bain. (2019)

The researchED Guide to Education Myths: An evidence-informed guide for teachers (The researchED series). Edited by Craig Barton. (2019)

How Learning Happens: Seminal Works in Educational Psychology and What They Mean in Practice. Carl Hendrick and Paul A. Kirschner. (2020)

CHAPTER 2
CURRICULUM DESIGN AND DEVELOPMENT

In the current education landscape the roles of curriculum and retrieval practice are widely referenced and discussed, which is a very good thing. They are not buzzwords or fads, in fact, curriculum design and retrieval practice are central to effective teaching and learning. It is important to see them as inextricably linked and complementary, and not doing so can lead to teachers and school leaders going astray with both.

Curriculum (to simplify) refers to the content that is taught. It is an umbrella term as it covers knowledge, vocabulary, concepts and skills that students need to understand, learn or be able to do. There can be a lot of terminology and jargon when it comes to curriculum, but author and former headteacher John Tomsett defines curriculum as, 'The stuff you want students to be able to know, understand and do by the time you have finished teaching them.' I like that description and find it helpful.

During initial teacher training/education (ITT/ITE) a trainee teacher is a novice in terms of curriculum. They will develop skills and knowledge on how to deliver the content of a curriculum supported by expertise from experienced teachers, leaders and mentors. But when does a teacher transition from novice to expert in terms of curriculum design? This cannot be achieved through experience alone (although that does help significantly) therefore there must be professional learning and development opportunities provided for all teachers and leaders at all levels that promotes ongoing dialogue and reflection with curriculum.

Although a curriculum will vary from setting to setting and there are many nuances to consider, schools can learn a lot from each other. As I have been fortunate enough to visit many primary schools across the UK and internationally, I have had the privilege to observe, listen, learn and ask questions. I would highly recommend school leaders reach out to other schools (either locally or further afield) to share, collaborate and learn with a focus on curriculum, and to do so regularly.

The diagram below was created and shared by Durrington Research School, a school well known for leading the way with their evidence-informed approach to teaching and learning, and is taken from their *Curriculum, Teaching and Assessment Policy.*

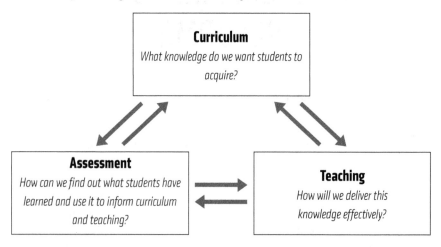

As the Durrington Research School blog explains:

We have invested our time and effort into this, because we feel there is a moral imperative for decisions about curriculum, teaching and assessment to be informed by the best available evidence and the practical wisdom of the most effective teachers. This has framed our policy. Curriculum, teaching and assessment are inextricably linked. When all three are aligned and of the highest quality, they should facilitate effective learning for all students, irrespective of their starting points. In turn, this should translate into all students making good progress and achieving strong academic outcomes. This matters, because it gives them the best possible life chances.[31]

I believe this is applicable and helpful for both primary and secondary schools. Curriculum design should be considered in the long-term, as Jon Hutchinson writes, 'Curriculum should be viewed over years, not in chunks of six weeks.'[32] This has been at the heart of a lot of

---

31   Durrington Research School (2018). Curriculum, teaching and assessment. *Find the bright spots.* Available at: https://classteaching.wordpress.com/2018/06/19/curriculum-teaching-and-assessment/

32   Sharma, L. (2020). *Curriculum to Classroom: A Handbook to Prompt Thinking Around Primary Curriculum Design and Delivery.* Woodbridge: John Catt. Page 60.

curriculum conversations I have had with primary school leaders that have shifted their focus, and planning and retrieval practice has played an integral role in this. Links and connections between different topics and subjects across the curriculum can provide useful and meaningful opportunities for relevant retrieval practice, supporting the encoding process with learning of new material as well as revisiting prior learning.

In the Ofsted *Education Inspection Framework*, it was clear that possible curricula were at the forefront in terms of the Ofsted focus. It was stated explicitly that inspectors would evaluate the extent to which, 'the provider's curriculum is coherently planned and sequenced towards cumulatively sufficient knowledge and skills for future learning and employment.' There was an explicit statement, too, that teaching should be designed to help learners remember, 'in the long-term the content they have been taught and to integrate new knowledge into larger concepts.'[33] Towards that goal, retrieval practice has a critical role to play in supporting students' ability to recall key facts and concepts in the long-term hence the importance of schools across England being able to effectively embed retrieval practice; not to appease Ofsted but to genuinely support learners with long-term learning, progression and confidence.

It is interesting to observe how the references and focus of cognitive science and psychology vary (or in some cases are absent) from official policy and documentation. I believe it is fair to say that outside of England the interest in retrieval practice has been from a school and grass roots level as opposed to acting on national policy or advice (unlike England where Ofsted, the DfE and the *Early Career Framework* (ECF) have all documented the importance of cognitive science, and specifically memory). This also highlights how many schools are further ahead in terms of being evidence-informed than the inspectorate and national government making decisions linked to education.

When designing a curriculum the focus naturally tends to be on 'what' needs to be included in the curriculum, which of course is very important. Linked to this question however, has to be the 'why'. What are the reasons and rationale for the decisions made with curriculum design and development? This can be addressed in the curriculum intent statement. Teacher and author Ruth Ashbee defines curriculum

---

33   Ofsted (2019). *Education Inspection Framework. Guidance*. Available at: https://www.gov. uk/government/publications/education-inspection-framework/education-inspection-framework

as the substance of what is taught, structured over time.[34] This element of structuring the curriculum is another essential element of curriculum design and can be supported by cognitive science.

The 'why' will be shaped by statutory requirements, for example at EYFS is the curriculum consistent with the educational programmes set out in the published *EYFS Statutory Framework*? The same will apply with the *Curriculum for Excellence in Scotland* and the *Curriculum for Wales*. The 'why' will also be shaped by the context and culture of the school environment.

In recent years there have been a lot of new terms and acronyms introduced to education policy and discourse. This is partly due to the cognitive science revolution taking place, with increased interest in and greater emphasis on evidence-informed strategies. There were already a lot of acronyms (they vary across the home nations too) and this can be challenging for teachers early in their career to grasp. In regard to curriculum and knowledge, it is necessary to be aware of the following terms which I have summarised briefly:

Substantive knowledge refers to the body of factual knowledge; the information and content within each specific subject. The substance of each subject. Substantive knowledge for subjects can be vast therefore teachers and leaders have to reflect on the substantive knowledge that is selected (and neglected) and how that is sequenced over time. Jasper Green, head of curriculum and assessment at Ark writes, 'Substantive knowledge, when it connects to more substantive knowledge, creates understanding. Relate this knowledge to what you already know and you will create meaning (or misconceptions!) – the Holy Grail for any teacher or curriculum.'[35]

In the study of history for example, within each period studied as a topic there will be substantive knowledge students need to learn. This substantive knowledge can include key events, dates, individuals and features. The **disciplinary knowledge** will be the study of historical sources of evidence, enquiry and interpretations. Disciplinary knowledge refers to the skills required to gain substantive knowledge therefore they go hand in hand.

---

34   Ashbee, R. (2021). *Curriculum: Theory, Culture and the Subject Specialisms*. Abingdon: Routledge. Page 14.

35   Green, J. (2017). Building a great curriculum – what knowledge do we need? *Ark online blog*. Available at: https://arkonline.org/blog/building-great-curriculum-what-knowledge-do-we-need#:~:text=There%20is%20substantive%20knowledge%20%E2%80%93%20this,the%20idea%20of%20a%20force.

There is also **experiential knowledge**, which focuses on knowledge gained through experience which lends itself to physical and practical subjects and EYFS.

This chapter specifically considers and explores the role of retrieval practice with curriculum design and development. What content to include (and exclude) from a curriculum and why are entirely different conversations, but what is included must become embedded and recallable, and for that retrieval practice is required.

We need to combine the 'what' with the 'how'. As Dylan Wiliam pointed out, "The problem is that a collection of learning materials is no more a curriculum than a pile of bricks is a house. What our students need are carefully organised, sequential, structured introductions to school subjects.'[36] Teachers and leaders should think very carefully about curriculum design not only with respect to organisational structure, but also with respect to how evidence–informed strategies can be incorporated to support the learning and retention of key concepts. There are a wide range of retrieval practice tasks that are easy to introduce and embed across lessons. However, we now need to take this a step further and consider what retrieval tasks might be used at different points in the curriculum and with different ages and key stages, and with different subjects and topics.

In order to go beyond simply doing retrieval practice tasks in lessons – perhaps sometimes ad hoc or infrequently – it is possible to carefully plan and sequence what target memories to focus on and consider the task and question design. Combining retrieval practice as an element of curriculum design encourages teachers to consider at what points in the curriculum and in lessons retrieval tasks should be carried out and what specifically should be recalled.

A common theme that emerged from my conversations with primary teachers and leaders was the concept of using retrieval practice as more than a starter or 'do now' task at the beginning of a lesson. I am an advocate for starting lessons with retrieval practice; there are many benefits of doing this as it becomes an established and effective classroom routine, it can settle students and focus the class on learning, which in itself provides an opportunity for recall, addressing areas of strength and areas to focus on. But retrieval practice should not just be

---

36   Wiliam, D. (2018). 2 simple changes to create the schools our children need. *Teachwire. net*. Available at: https://www.teachwire.net/news/2-simple-changes-to-create-the-schools-our-children-need

used at the start of a lesson. It is a well known and effective teaching and learning strategy, so to limit and restrict it to five minutes per lesson is a wasted opportunity.

Science teacher, author and co-creator of Carousel Learning, Adam Boxer explains in his fascinating and insightful book *Teaching Secondary Science: A Complete Guide* how there are four major opportunities for teachers to execute retrieval practice at different points of the learning process, both inside and outside the classroom.[37] Although Boxer is a secondary specialist, I believe these four retrieval opportunities are applicable at primary too:

1. **Fixed-point quizzing** – This involves routine quizzes based on prior learning carried out at the start of a lesson. Boxer points out that this retrieval practice alone is not sufficient, and I agree. Further opportunities are required for regular retrieval practice.

2. **Questioning before and during explanations** – This involves asking students questions on prerequisite knowledge in order to develop links and ensure they are ready to progress to learning new content.

3. **While students are practising** – Boxer writes, 'Interleaving questions while students are practising is an excellent opportunity to introduce retrieval, break algorithmic problem solving and show the interconnectedness of topics.'

4. **Homework** – This will vary for different year groups at primary but the sooner we encourage families to support their child with quizzing and regular retrieval practice at home, the better.

Homework should be considered carefully as part of curriculum design and implementation. This can be seized as another opportunity to support long-term learning. Stanley Road Primary School, in Oldham, communicates very clearly to parents and carers about the expectations and purpose of homework at their school. The homework information on the school website states:

> At Stanley Road, we think that it is important for children to practise what they have learned in class at home to help them to be the best that they can be – our homework gives them the opportunity to do this. In years 2–6, homework will be provided for pupils on Google Classroom and all resources they may need will be put on the

---

37 Boxer, A. (2021). *Teaching Secondary Science: A Complete Guide*. Woodbridge: John Catt. Page 344.

Classroom. Pupils will be given their login details, if your child does not have a login please talk to their class teacher.

Here are the expectations for homework in KS1 and 2 –

Reading – We expect all pupils to read at home (or be read to) every day. A record of this is then kept in the child's reading record book.

Spelling – We expect pupils to learn a small set of spellings each week. This is best completed in short bursts over the course of the week.

Mathematics – We expect all pupils to practise recalling their number facts (including number bonds and times tables) for a few minutes each day. One useful resource for parents of KS2 children is the Times Tables Rock Stars website that your child can log in to. There may also be short maths tasks put on Google Classroom to support learning in class.

Other Subjects – We expect pupils to learn the information on the Knowledge Organiser sheet which is sent home each half term. A schedule is provided to show which sections should be learned each week. Pupils will be tested on this in school and we expect them to know this core information off by heart. In years 2–6, teachers will provide tasks on Google Classroom to support your child in learning their Knowledge Organiser.

Poetry Recital Performances – We expect pupils to learn a number of poems to present in assemblies over the year. These will be sent home so parents can help their children learn these by heart. Please see the calendar page on the website for details of when these assemblies take place.

Additional Homework – For pupils in years 2–6, there will be a bank of additional resources provided on their Google Classroom. Teachers may provide videos, tasks or links to home learning resources such as: National Oak Academy, Purple Mash and BBC Bitesize. These additional resources are curated to match the Stanley Road curriculum and offer revision of content pupils have studied in school.

At Stanley Road, we believe it is vital for children to learn significant information 'by heart' so that it makes learning in the future much easier. This is best done in short bursts each day rather than spending time on long pieces of homework once a week. If you have any further questions about homework please speak to your child's class teacher. If your child has special educational needs we will adapt homework to suit them if this is needed. Also, if your child ever receives any homework which you feel is too difficult or it is not clear what to do then please speak to the class teacher. While we do expect children to complete all homework, we do not want this to be a source of anxiety for you or your children.[38]

I think this is communicated very well and I have been to Stanley Road Primary School to observe the lessons and culture of learning that is evident within every classroom from EYFS to Year 6.

There can also be lessons which are solely dedicated to retrieval practice. A pause session or retrieve and reflect lesson can allow for meaningful retrieval practice, elaboration, feedback and reflection as well as guiding future planning for the teacher. This will need to be carefully planned and it should be agreed in advance among teachers and leaders, at which point in the curriculum it should happen. This is an approach I have embedded with all my classes and takes place once per half term after a significant amount of content and retrieval practice has already taken place. Introducing this does have an impact on curriculum time, especially with so many subjects at primary. In a primary context I would advise to do this regularly with core subjects and alternate each half term with foundation subjects.

It also became clear from dialogue with teachers and leaders and my observations in schools, that there are different levels of consistency. Some schools are at the point of introducing retrieval practice and others are more confident in terms of it being embedded across the curriculum. Based on my own experiences as a teacher and middle leader I have devised an evidence-informed suggested five-step plan towards achieving the goal of embedding retrieval practice across the curriculum. This is not by any means fixed and some schools I have worked with have followed this model exactly whereas others have simply taken elements from it and adapted them to suit their context, while applying the principles of being evidence-informed.

Boxer does stress the importance of creating a culture of retrieval within a school and despite the challenges of doing this, it is fundamentally worth it. Boxer writes, 'Building a culture of retrieval is one of the hardest things you can do as a teacher, as it requires such careful forethought, strong knowledge of your subjects, strong knowledge of your students, a powerful and useful platform and a fair amount of trial and error.' Again, I wholeheartedly agree. A key message to remember is that in the same way learning happens over

---

38   Stanley Road Primary School (2022). School Website. Available at: https://www.stanleyroad.oldham.sch.uk/homework.html

time, embedding effective retrieval practice across the curriculum also happens over time.

1. The first step focuses on:
Establishing essential knowledge and skills.

A key question for every leader and teacher to focus on and discuss with their colleagues is:

'What are the essential elements of the curriculum students need to know and be able to do?'

This question has to be the starting point with curriculum design. However, although the question is the starting point, the answer will need to cover the end point as well, and all points in between the two. It will consider what children should be able to know and do at the end of a topic, year and/or key stage. What are the intended target memories? Once this question has been discussed, explored, and answered (with likely lots more questions to be considered) a curriculum can be planned. This is difficult and needs time, it cannot just be discussed in one single meeting or inset day.

The challenges will vary with the contexts; an EYFS curriculum will have different priorities and foci in comparison to key stage 2 (KS2). What is expected from each subject and topic and each year group? This needs to be explicitly clear and shared among colleagues. A Year 6 teacher should have a strong grasp and knowledge of content that has been taught previously. I am sure primary teachers have this grasp but when curriculum changes are made it can be difficult to have in-depth knowledge and insight of changes outside the classes taught. As a secondary history teacher, I knew exactly what my Year 9 classes had studied in Years 7 and 8 because I taught those lessons, which is an advantage primary teachers don't have, unless they have taught a year group previously and moved up with them, but this is not common.

In order to truly understand the essential elements of a curriculum, it is important to consider those elements that are not deemed essential. Beyond any acquisition of basic content there is information that is useful to cover because it provides background knowledge or, perhaps, is simply interesting and promotes the curiosity and creativity which play such an important role in the primary classroom. It is important, though, to nail down what the essentials are, that is, the core concepts, subject specific vocabulary and as Tomsett stated, the stuff that students must know. Every curriculum should be ambitious for every child, so the essential knowledge isn't simply the basics, it is the very essence of an ambitious curriculum for all.

I have categorised different types of knowledge as the following:

1. Non-essential knowledge
2. Essential knowledge
3. Desirable knowledge

What is non-essential knowledge?

It could be argued that a curriculum shouldn't contain any information or knowledge that isn't essential; but such information can serve a purpose. It could simply be relevant information that is interesting and engaging. I have been known when teaching lessons to share fun facts that I have read or can recall from a museum visit or a holiday. This is information I want to share with my students because ultimately I do want to share my knowledge and passion for the subjects and content I teach, with the hope that my students will develop that same intrigue and interest too.

What does this have to do with retrieval practice? Curriculum plans (schemes of work, for example) cover content, vocabulary and concepts in which the essentials are distinguished from trivia and background content. If it's not essential then it shouldn't be included in a retrieval task or as a recall question; it's not the target memory.

An example of such non-essential information being asked, was a question in an online quiz about the date Henry VIII was born. I can recall many key dates in history, but I could not answer this question at that moment in time. On reflection I realised the dates I can recall with speed and accuracy include the dates monarchs reigned or when key legislation was passed. They are dates of significance within the curriculum, which is not true of the year Henry VIII was born. Do students really need to know the date in terms of day, month and year that Henry VIII was born?

I would argue that knowing the dates Henry VIII ruled is more significant and important, although this is dependent on the content and context of the curriculum, as some may consider his birth to be significant perhaps in the context of Henry VII, but that's another discussion focusing on the 'what'. This type of question could be heading into territory known as 'pub quiz trivia' which should be avoided.

The curriculum must go beyond factual recall of dates so these will need to be explicitly linked to chronology, causation and other elements of subject specific curriculum design. If we quiz students on non-essential information, for example the year a monarch was born, it is likely that knowledge will stick. This could be viewed as harmless, but there is evidence that remembering such harmless information can interfere with the likelihood that more important information is recallable.

Cognitive scientists have demonstrated what Anderson, Bjork, and Bjork labelled 'retrieval induced forgetting'[39] which refers to the fact that when we recall something from our memories we not only make that something more recallable in the future, but also make information that might compete with that information less recallable. Basically, as teachers we have to accept that students will not remember everything we tell them – to put it mildly – so we need to focus on what they need to remember, both for its own sake and as a foundation for further learning.

Another example from my own teaching experience was creating a quiz for my class about the events of 1066. I had written 16 questions and wanted to round it up to 20 (as students tend to answer multiple-choice questions relatively quickly we can include a greater number of questions) so I added another question which asked:

Q) What is the name of the historian in the video clip we watched?

A) Simon Schama

B) Dan Snow

C) Haili Rubenhold

D) I don't know yet

The answer was Dan Snow, but did my students really need to be able to know that and recall his name? The key individuals they must be able to recall information about are the contenders to the throne in 1066. If students can recall Dan Snow, that isn't a problem but if I have included that in a quiz they may assume (and understandably so) that it is essential they learn the name of Dan Snow; but it really isn't.

---

39   Anderson, M. C., Bjork, R. and Bjork, E. L. (1994). Remembering can cause forgetting: Retrieval dynamics in long-term memory. *Journal of Experimental Psychology-Learning Memory and Cognition*, 20, 1063-1087.

After reading about retrieval induced forgetting, I then revisited previous quizzes I had created and decided to remove questions that focused on non-essential information (often filler style questions like the Dan Snow example). I realised this was something I was doing a lot; adding questions testing non-essential knowledge. Fewer questions in my quizzes meant more time for feedback and reflection or for delivering new content.

Essential knowledge refers to everything on the curriculum that students need to know and should be able to do. We will only be sure students know this information if they can recall it from long-term memory. Many schools use knowledge organisers (KOs) as shown below in the example created by primary teacher and leader Adam Woodward (KOs are discussed in detail in chapter 4).

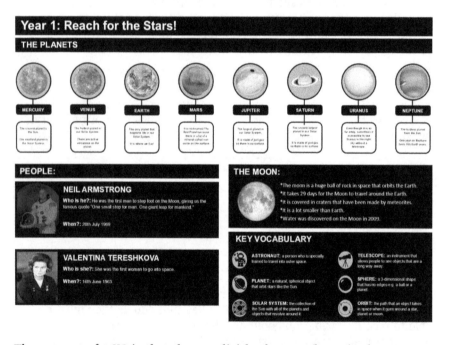

The concept of a KO is that they explicitly show students (and parents and carers) what the essential knowledge and content is. It is condensed information; it can include concepts, facts, dates, individuals, terminology, illustrations and more. It should show students what will be taught and what they are expected to learn, meaning recall from long-term memory through retrieval. It should only contain the essential information; that's one of the main points to be aware of when designing and using a KO.

Desirable knowledge is certainly part of an ambitious and knowledge rich curriculum. It refers to content that, while it could be argued isn't absolutely essential, is relevant and would further strengthen knowledge and understanding and develop responses with extra detail, depth, richness and mastery. It is important to have a shared understanding as to what the essential and desirable knowledge and elements are. That shared understanding should involve school leaders, teachers, students and their families.

Essential knowledge is the body of the curriculum that will be the target memories students will need to be able to recall from long-term memory. These target memories are therefore made up of knowledge all students should be able to recall. Non-essential knowledge can serve a purpose to provide some context or promote interest, but will not be required to be recallable. With the desirable knowledge, ideally we would like all students to be able to recall it, but some will struggle, just as some will struggle with the core content which has to take priority to ensure it is understood by all and recallable by all.

2. The second step is to ensure there are a range of:

Low effort, high impact retrieval techniques.

Establishing essential knowledge and skills has to be consistent across a school but the second step promotes teacher autonomy and flexibility as to how the content and skills are taught. 'Low effort, high impact' has become my mantra with lesson planning in general, and specifically with retrieval practice. It has become an important element in terms of task design and delivery in my classroom.

The 'low effort' part should be from the teacher's perspective. Spending hours creating, cutting and laminating teaching resources requires a lot of teacher effort, but does not by itself guarantee the high impact on learning that should be the focus of those efforts. I am an advocate for careful and considerate question design, hence the term is low effort not no effort. It is important teachers invest their efforts to ensure a high impact with learning will be achieved.

There are a huge number of retrieval practice templates available online including multiple choice quizzes, cued recall (retrieval practice with prompts and cues to support recall) and free recall (no support provided). Teachers do not need to keep reinventing the wheel when there exist high impact resources and tools that can be used repeatedly. A teacher's efforts can then be invested in the design of questions that induce productive retrieval practice, including modifying those questions in ways that produce productive retrieval practice for students who are at different levels of comprehension of lesson and content materials.

Retrieval practice across the curriculum has to be low effort for teachers otherwise it simply will not be sustainable, and it needs to be sustainable if it is to become a regular classroom routine and norm. In addition, the more regular the retrieval practice, the lower the stakes, as students recognise and understand it is a teaching and learning strategy not a high stakes assessment strategy.

This low effort is something that teachers should be aware of and self-regulate, but leaders at all levels should also be mindful of this, ensuring retrieval practice is not negatively impacting teacher workload.

If designing, delivering and providing feedback on retrieval practice tasks becomes a workload issue then this needs to change. Dylan Wiliam previously offered this advice to teachers, 'The best person to mark a test is the person who has just taken the test.'[40] Retrieval practice lends itself very well to self-assessment, as well as a host of online tools and websites that will provide instant feedback to students. Self-assessment can be done with younger students for retrieval based tasks when answers are presented and communicated clearly with teacher guidance and monitoring.

3. The third step:
Consider the school calendar when designing a curriculum.

This is often not considered, and it wasn't something I thought about as a teacher and middle leader until reading the work of Bjork and Bjork in *The New Theory of Disuse.*[41] There will be specific points in the academic year where it is advisable to carry out a review and refresher of previous material instead of a retrieval practice task. Such times can include when students return to school after a holiday, during which it is highly unlikely they have revisited the course content covered earlier.

---

40 Hendrick, C. and Macpherson, R. (2017). *What does this look like in the classroom? Bridging the gap between research and practice.* Woodbridge: John Catt.

41 Bjork, R. and Bjork, E. (1992). A new theory of disuse and an old theory of stimulus fluctuation. *Essays in honor of William K. Estes, Vol. 1991: From learning theory to connectionist theory.* 1935-1967.

Another consideration is that a retrieval practice task administered at the start of a term will not tend to accurately reflect what students have learned because information that is not recallable may exist in a student's memory and come back readily when presented again. Linked to this is advice offered by myself, Robert A. Bjork and Dylan Wiliam published by the ASCD, 'It might be tempting to test our students as soon as they return to the classroom but doing so is likely to be an unpleasant experience for students and provide little meaningful information for teachers. Instead, we propose that prior to assessing the levels of pandemic-related learning loss, teachers should first carry out a refresher review of previously learned material. Doing so will increase both retrieval strength and storage strength, and at the same time, give students confidence that what they used to know has not been forgotten but is still there, waiting to be reactivated'.[42]

There is a need then to distinguish between what Bjork and Bjork refer to in their *New Theory of Disuse* as storage strength, and retrieval strength. American psychologist Edward Thorndike published *The Law of Use and Disuse* in 1914 which suggested that the less an association or piece of information from memory is used, the weaker it becomes, and thus memories can decay. This theory by Thorndike dominated the thinking of researchers and educators for many years in terms of forgetting. There was a belief that if you don't use it (referring to a memory) then you lose it forever.

This was later discredited, and Bjork and Bjork were able to demonstrate that information that has been transferred to long-term memory but not accessed in a long time, does not become lost but instead becomes inaccessible. It can be inaccessible but still remain in memory. Robert A. Bjork has stated that understanding of this is 'crucial in terms of how human memory works'.[43]

Storage strength refers to how well learned something is, as defined by how inter-associated it is with related facts and concepts in a student's memory. Retrieval strength is a measure of how accessible that something is at a current time and in a particular setting, meaning that it is very sensitive to recency and the degree to which the current

42 Bjork, R. A., Jones, K. and Wiliam, D. (2022). *Why testing shouldn't be the first response to last year's learning gaps*. ASCD. Available at: https://www.ascd.org/el/articles/why-testing-shouldnt-be-the-first-response-to-last-years-learning-gaps

43 Bjork, R. A. (ND). *Applying cognitive psychology to enhance educational practice*. UCLA Bjork Learning and Forgetting Lab. Available at: https://bjorklab.psych.ucla.edu/research/#ntd

context provides cues to that memory. I believe this to be vital to understanding learning, yet it is still not widely known among the teaching profession. This has to change.

Knowledge that has been stored in one's brain does not fade away with disuse, like footprints in the sand, but instead becomes inaccessible, except in the presence of distinctive and discriminating cues. Something can be well learned from a storage strength standpoint, but be non-recallable at a particular time in a particular context. Critically though, information that is high in storage strength becomes very accessible in the retrieval strength sense once re-presented or recalled.

Retrieval strength (unlike storage strength) can and does fluctuate. After a school holiday, a break from learning or significant amount of time since a topic was last revisited or quizzed, it is likely the retrieval strength of students will be low. Teachers and students shouldn't panic or fear, because a refresher or review of the material will provide a boost and increase the retrieval strength. This might involve a class discussion, revisiting prior work or referring to a knowledge organiser. This reminder of knowledge increases the retrieval strength.

Another reason it is important for teachers and leaders to be aware of retrieval strength is because when we set quizzes or tasks, and ask questions, if students are unable to perform well it can impact their confidence, morale and motivation. When retrieval strength is low and information is difficult to access this can knock the confidence of all those involved, both the student and the teacher. Conversely, after a review and refresh there is a greater chance of retrieval success, which can lead to increased confidence, morale and motivation.

4. Step four:

Establish links and connections across a long-term curriculum plan.

There are lots of legitimate questions teachers have about the details of how retrieval practice should be introduced and scheduled for which there are not good, or at least precise, answers. Teachers often ask me:

- How long should I spend on a retrieval task in a given lesson?
- How long should I wait to carry out a retrieval practice task with my class after teaching new content?
- How long should I spend on feedback in a lesson after retrieval practice?

There are simply too many variables to give specific answers to the questions above. What can be said with confidence is that, as teachers, we should make sure that we factor time into our curriculum for regular retrieval practice and provide time for meaningful feedback and reflection after sessions of retrieval practice.

Primary schools' curriculums have a degree of flexibility despite the difficult decisions to be made about what content to include or exclude. This flexibility enables regular retrieval practice to be built into a curriculum with a 'less is more' approach to content. There can be a tension between breadth and depth of content when designing a curriculum and again this links to retrieval practice because while we want students to have a breadth of knowledge it has to go beyond the surface to deep learning.

5. The final step, as with any approach to curriculum design: Review and reflection.

Curriculum design is never a finished task, as we are always reflecting, learning and developing. The goal of continual reflection and review is that we make changes to improve and enhance the curriculum. Reflection is a key element of curriculum design and should be carried out in collaboration with colleagues who are also teaching and delivering the curriculum.

I created the jigsaw infographic below to illustrate the main methods teachers can use to improve, develop and learn, and the four pieces can apply just as well to curriculum design. We can learn from others, whether in our own or other schools. Research can help to shape and inform the decisions made to design and develop an evidence-informed curriculum. Experiences in the classroom are key, even more so if we reflect on them and use those reflections to 'stick' with what works or change with a 'twist' to further improve.

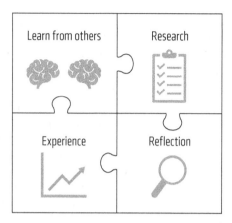

There are lots of questions and reflections to consider with retrieval practice and curriculum design that should be asked and discussed, those below are just a small sample:

- Is retrieval practice having an impact? How do we know this?
- Are there any noticeable benefits from using retrieval practice?
- Are there any challenges with retrieval practice?
- Are students embracing retrieval practice?
- How have parents/carers responded to retrieval practice?
- Are the techniques being used low effort and high impact?
- How are students responding to retrieval practice?
- Are retrieval practice tasks taking too long in a lesson?
- Has there been a significant improvement in outcomes?
- Has there been disruption to learning and the school calendar that has had an impact on the curriculum?
- Is the curriculum effective in preparing children for the next key stage/phase of their learning?
- What needs improvement?
- What are our next steps?

Case study: Stick or twist with curriculum design? Lekha Sharma.

I am delighted to be able to include a case study in this chapter by Lekha Sharma, a leading expert in primary curriculum design. I thoroughly enjoyed reading *Curriculum to Classroom: A Handbook to Prompt Thinking Around Primary Curriculum Design and Delivery* by Lekha and I highly recommend it.

A very real tension exists in curricular development – on the one hand educators aim to maintain the integrity of the curriculum so that it is not constantly shifting and leaving gaps in understanding, and on the other hand educators aspire to continuously refine their school curriculum to strengthen it over time. It's a difficult but important balance to achieve and it is widely accepted that curriculum work is never really 'finished'.

Maintaining the integrity of the curriculum we commit to deliver is important so that curriculum coherence can be achieved. If learners are studying The Great Fire of London, as they often do in Year 2, it's important that they understand that London is the capital city of the United Kingdom ahead of this, which they may learn in Year 1, offering them crucial context. If units of study are constantly changing, this golden thread of understanding is lost. This, however, is distinct from the process of refining the curriculum to strengthen it over time.

Refining the curriculum might take many forms and is likely to be informed by the actual delivery of the curriculum. Once the curriculum has been delivered to students, we can take a step back and make some intentional choices to strengthen the delivery and sometimes in part, the design. For example, you may decide that a unit of study is better suited towards the end of the year once prior knowledge is established through a different unit of study. You may refine how you're delivering a given unit of work based on your experiences of teaching it on the ground. These tweaks, much like the formative assessment that informs lesson planning, helps us to inform our subsequent curricular plans and allow us to narrow the inevitable discrepancy between the intended and enacted curriculum.

A way you might wish to do this is through an annual or termly curriculum review, where teachers come together with annotated copies of the curriculum and share how they would adapt it going forward. Collective and collaborative review of the curriculum can be a powerful way to decide how the curriculum will be improved going forward. It also allows teachers to engage and be involved in top-level curriculum design, cultivating ownership and agency. Alternatively, you may wish to look at great artefacts and outcomes of the curriculum and share the materials, planning and resources that led to these. These benchmarks of brilliance can support teachers in developing their pedagogy. However you choose to engage in what I like to call 'curriculum kaizen' or an approach to curriculum improvement focused on small incremental steps, taking that all-important step back to review the curriculum is crucial. It gives us a sense of the overall curriculum picture and how this translates on the ground in classrooms.

I liken this process of stepping back to the phenomenon that astronauts experience when they go into space and see the Earth as a whole – the overview effect. Astronauts report that when they see the Earth as a whole, they have an experience of seeing things from a different perspective that they don't quite have when they're on Earth and are so absorbed in it all. Similarly, when we're in the thick of it and delivering a lesson on a rainy Thursday afternoon, we tend to be so absorbed in our lesson, that we don't necessarily have the headspace to review the unit and reflect on how it fits in with the bigger picture of the wider curriculum. Carving out time for colleagues to come together to do so is an important investment in terms of quality assuring what happens on the ground day-to-day.

Thank you to Lekha Sharma for sharing her expertise and advice. You can follow Lekha on Twitter @teacherfeature2 and visit her teaching and learning blog https://teacherfeature2.com/.

Many schools across the UK are embracing retrieval practice and are keen to learn more about how it can support and enhance their curriculum. Retrieval practice and curriculum design and development are not just hot topics in the UK but in schools around the world. I taught internationally in the United Arab Emirates for six years. During that time I worked hard to share as widely as possible research, reflections and advice as to how the curriculum and lessons can be effective through being evidence-informed. I and many others began leading the way towards an international evidence-informed movement.

The aim is not about cramming as much content and as many opportunities for factual recall into a curriculum as possible, but instead carefully selecting the knowledge and skills to be taught, and planning for opportunities to check at a later date whether that knowledge has been understood and remains recallable. There are other cognitive science principles that can be linked to curriculum design, including cognitive load theory, spaced practice and interleaving. Again, these are context dependent and linked to retrieval practice. Leaders and teachers at all levels play an essential role in curriculum design, ensuring it is both knowledge rich and evidence-informed.

Further recommended reading

Curriculum to Classroom: A Handbook to Prompt Thinking Around Primary Curriculum Design and Delivery. Lekha Sharma. (2020)

Symbiosis: The Curriculum and the Classroom. Kat Howard and Claire Hill. (2020)

ResearchED Guide to The Curriculum: An Evidence-informed Guide for Teachers. Edited by Clare Sealy. Series Editor Tom Bennett. (2020)

Primary Huh: Curriculum conversations with subject leaders in primary schools. Mary Myatt and John Tomsett. (2022)

CHAPTER 3
KNOWLEDGE ORGANISERS

Knowledge organisers (KOs) have become widely used as a popular classroom resource to support learning. If you are using a KO in school hopefully this chapter will provide lots of advice as to how they can be fully utilised both inside and outside of the classroom. If you have not used a KO before then I would encourage you to consider it as a learning resource. This chapter can guide you in terms of creation, design, distribution and use.

The idea of a KO is credited to former Michaela Community School senior leader and English teacher Joe Kirby.[44] It was created as a resource for secondary students but has been embraced by primary schools too. For anyone unfamiliar with the concept of a KO here is a description by Kirby:

> *A knowledge curriculum specifies, in meticulous detail, the exact facts, dates, events, characters, concepts and precise definitions that pupils are expected to master in long-term memory. ... The most powerful tool in the arsenal of the curriculum designer is the knowledge organiser. These organise all the most vital, useful and powerful knowledge on a single page.*

Kirby explains that they are useful because they provide clarity for teachers and memory for pupils. I have also encountered KOs referred to as knowledge banks, knowledge specifications, memory mats and summary sheets. A lot of teachers and leaders agree with Kirby about the value of a KO, although not everyone shares that enthusiasm for them.

It is worth adding what a KO is not. It's not a curriculum or scheme of work but those will inspire and inform the creation of a KO. Due to the interest and focus on a knowledge rich curriculum in recent years, it is easy to see why this resource has such appeal and has gained significant attention.

A KO has many benefits for school leaders, classroom teachers, students and their families. It is a document that contain an overview of the

---

44   Kirby, J. (2015). Knowledge Organisers. *Pragmatic Reform*. Available at: https://prag-maticreform.wordpress.com/2015/03/28/knowledge-organisers/

essentials; core knowledge ranging from vocabulary, concepts, dates, individuals and more. This provides a shared understanding for school leaders, teachers, students and their families as to what the essential knowledge is. A KO can support consistency across a school (if all staff use them in a similar manner) and can provide consistency for students across year groups and subjects. They can be used to actively encourage parents and carers to be more involved with the learning of their child and be used for meaningful home learning.

The issues, pitfalls and limitations of using a knowledge organiser

The idea and concept of a KO is great, but their effective implementation can be challenging to achieve. There are many schools that have created, embedded and shared their KOs within the school community and are noticing the visible benefits and impact whereas other schools and teachers have not quite reached that point yet. As mentioned, Kirby is a secondary specialist, so we have to ask about the use and application of a KO in a primary context. Questions worth asking and reflecting on include:

- Are they effective for all ages/year groups?
- Are they effective for all subjects?
- How can they be used with primary students both inside and outside of the classroom?
- What are the benefits for primary students, teachers, leaders and families in the school community?
- What are the barriers or issues for primary students, teachers, leaders and families in the school community?
- How should they be created and designed?
- How and when should they be shared with students?
- Does the KO provide opportunities for further elaboration?

Neil Almond is an advocate for using KOs in primary schools. He describes a KO as, 'a summary of key facts and essential knowledge'[45] and adds that a KO should include, 'information broken down into easily digestible chunks.' A key message that Almond shares, echoing that of Kirby and others, is that it is vital to only include what is absolutely crucial; this can be easier said than done as a big challenge can be

---

45   Almond, N. (2020). Knowledge organisers: what they are and how to use them In KS1 and KS2. *Third Space Learning*. Available at: https://thirdspacelearning.com/blog/knowledge-organisers/

figuring out what the core content and essentials are (as discussed in chapter 2 as part of curriculum design). A KO can become overcrowded and contain far too much information crammed onto an A4 document. This is why it lends itself to a topic or theme per term or half term rather than a whole subject per year, it is more manageable and realistic.

Author and EEF National Content Manager Alex Quigley has written about KOs stating that teachers, 'have to recognise that KOs lend themselves to facts: word lists, definitions, dates and so on. Students can therefore develop an illusion of knowledge from just a few key facts.' He continues, 'Yet understanding how to apply that knowledge to a complex task, such as a piece of extended writing, is another thing entirely.'[46] This links to the learning process with encoding, storage and retrieval but we must not forget the role of application and transfer.

Concerns teachers may have when it comes to creating and using a KO can include:

- How do I fit everything onto one side of A4?
- How do I decide what to include and exclude?
- How do I design a clearly laid out and effective KO?
- I don't know how to design a KO or make it look good.
- Creating a KO will take too much time, effort and energy.
- I already have textbooks, can't I use them or photocopy pages instead?
- What if we change or adapt the curriculum, will I have to create another KO from scratch?
- Are the KOs available online high quality?
- There are too many subjects and topics to create a KO for!
- Is this another fad that will be dismissed in a few years?

These are understandable concerns, hence the need for careful consideration about how to introduce, implement and embed knowledge organisers across the curriculum.

Creation and design of a KO

A KO can and should be used as a retrieval practice tool, but before I discuss that, it is worth exploring their creation, design and how

---

46   Quigley, A. (2021). *Do knowledge organisers help students learn?* TES, October 2021. Available at: https://www.tes.com/magazine/teaching-learning/general/do-knowledge-organisers-help-students-learn

to communicate their use within and across the school community. It is worth keeping in mind that a KO should be designed to support quizzing and retrieval tasks. To do this requires information to be organised in a way that means a KO can be folded over or allow information to be hidden for quizzing, then easily revealed to provide the correct answers. Bullet points and lists are more suited to a KO than lengthy paragraphs. Diagrams, sequences and timelines all lend themselves well, but they must focus on essential knowledge.

There are many ready made KOs available online for teachers, including the TES and Twinkl websites. Some are freely available and others require payment. Naturally, the quality varies significantly. I have spoken to schools where staff have used a paid subscription to purchase and download a KO whereas other schools have asked staff to create their own. I am not stating which I think is the right or wrong option because there are pros and cons to both approaches.

In terms of purchasing or freely downloading a KO online; this does save time and effort and can be a positive aspect in terms of workload, especially considering how many topics and subjects are taught at primary. There are some KOs online that look visually impressive as they have been created by experienced teachers and a professional design team; which could be difficult for a teacher to replicate. However, this can rob teachers of a great planning opportunity to extend and develop their subject knowledge and promote thinking carefully and deeply about curriculum content.

It is critical if schools are asking staff to create a KO from scratch that guidance and time is provided. This could be in terms of providing a template, modelling or sharing good examples in addition to dedicated time during an inset day or meeting. Even when creating your own KO it is a useful activity to view others online or from colleagues as this can provide guidance, inspiration or possibly show how to not to do it! A good idea in terms of creating a KO is to promote collaboration. This could involve teams, subject leaders or colleagues across a trust, and promotes professional dialogue and supports teacher workload. Another idea would be to focus on introducing and embedding a KO within one subject or topic then gradually aiming to expand across the curriculum (as explained in the case study below).

Creating and designing a KO takes considerable time and effort. It should be considered as an investment to support teaching planning, in class support and a method of promoting retrieval practice both inside and outside of the classroom. As with any workload and time heavy task it's worth asking if the juice worth the squeeze. A personalised and carefully crafted KO will be wasted if it is simply glued inside a book and looks pretty but is not utilised effectively or fully.

Case study: Creating a knowledge organiser by Adam Woodward.

I spoke to the director of studies at Radnor House School, Adam Woodward about KOs he has created for his colleagues and shared on Twitter. I was very impressed with the clear layout and consistency across year groups and wanted to learn more about this process. Adam explains in this case study how his school has introduced the KO.

Knowledge organisers were introduced as a part of an initiative to promote retrieval practice across the school. This decision was made and the initiative launched after the first lockdown in 2020. It gave teachers an opportunity to trial their use within the classroom and feed back on the impact. It was important teachers were not overloaded with an increased workload, therefore we limited the introduction of knowledge organisers within our curriculum by making the decision to trial in some subjects before implementing KOs across all subjects. It is vital to take into consideration workload and wellbeing, as they go hand in hand, and creating a KO does require an investment of time and work.

While searching for the ideal template to support retrieval practice, I came across an example by Laura Healy @AHT_Mrs_ Healy. The examples Laura shared were clear, visually attractive, concise and exactly what I felt would benefit the children in our school setting. With this template, I was able to adapt this to create my own based on the needs of our children and content based on our curriculum.

After creating my own examples for our first history units for teachers across key stages 1 and 2, the feedback was very positive from both teachers and children. We had sent them home as a part of our parent bulletin so that they could be printed and 'stuck on the fridge'. We communicated with parents about the benefits of short bursts of information contained within our knowledge organisers and how this learning strategy would be beneficial within the classroom.

The introduction of these has been gradual within our curriculum, focusing on history and geography initially. The formation of a new knowledge organiser begins with teachers sharing the key information that they would like to impart to their students in their next unit. This includes key dates, key events, important individuals and the links to prior learning. These are examples of what information is passed onto me. It is then my job to create these for the class teachers.

The logic for me creating them rather than class teachers is for several reasons. Firstly, it means that I am not adding to teachers' workload – this is important for the use and application of knowledge organisers to be successful. It gives teachers time to spend creating quality resources to support the teaching and learning within these units. I have additional time to do so as part of my leadership role.

Creating the knowledge organisers for staff also ensures that I can monitor the consistency of them across the school. One of the key aspects to our knowledge organisers is the element of dual coding within them. Oliver Caviglioli explains that dual coding – combining words with images – stimulates the retrieval of the other, which, in turn, reduces the cognitive load within students, therefore, increasing the capacity of working memory (*Dual Coding with Teachers*, 2019). By ensuring that the same icons and images are being used for key vocabulary or substantive concepts within units across the school, children are able to embed their understanding further as they come across the icon and associated vocabulary more frequently.

As I am responsible for their creation, I can ensure that the use of images is consistent. If teachers were responsible, there is the possibility that different icons could be used in different parts of the school, thus not forming as much of a secure schema.

After their creation, they are distributed to children and referred to at the beginning of each history or geography lesson as well as being sent home to parents. Teachers plan in retrieval tasks using these regularly – multiple choice questioning for example – and children use these tasks to identify what information they have 'learned' and are confident in, and what they could spend more time learning going forward, with the aim that all information on the knowledge organiser will have been covered and learned by the end of the unit. All of this is of a low stakes level and supportive of the learning process.

At our school, retrieval practice is still in its infancy, due to the impact and disruption of the pandemic; limiting our chances to use and apply this regularly until the current academic year. However, teachers and children have responded well to them, and retrieval tasks planned within lessons show links to prior learning that promotes success within the classroom. An understanding of the progression of knowledge and skills that takes place within our history and geography curriculums is evident. The use of knowledge organisers has supported this and supports teachers with the outcomes of these units. There is still more to be done, but the continued implementation of this with our parents is something that we are looking to explore further, giving the wider school community a greater understanding of the benefits of retrieval practice, cognitive load theory and knowledge organisers in particular.

The expansion of the use of knowledge organisers into other areas of the curriculum is also something that we, as a school, are looking to move towards. Science, mathematics and religious education are some subject areas that have been discussed with regards to their use. However, we are realistic in the understanding that it is important to embed their use within history and geography first before expanding – making sure we don't run before we can walk. For anyone introducing knowledge organisers into their curriculum, this is not something that should be overlooked and taking time for implementation and reflection is key.

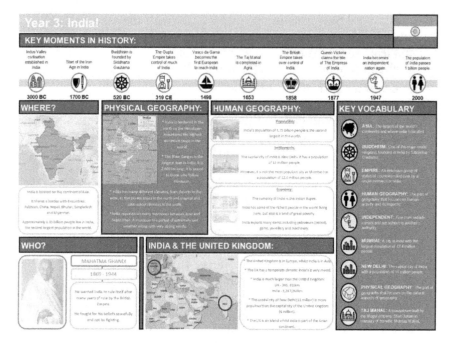

Thank you to Adam Woodward for his contribution and sharing how his school has approached the introduction of knowledge organisers. You can follow Adam on Twitter @ adamjames317.

When to share a knowledge organiser

To revisit the original post by Kirby about the use of a KO, he explains that they are, 'given to all pupils at the start of each unit to help them remember what they're learning.' This makes sense and we can understand the logic and benefits, but this is where I would suggest that primary teachers use a KO differently from their secondary colleagues. When to give students a KO and send it home will ultimately depend on its purpose, whether it is for encoding and retrieval practice or with more of an emphasis solely on retrieval practice. In terms of sharing a KO, I would advise primary teachers not to give it to their students at the start of the topic but instead at the end of a topic or unit, once all the content has been taught. I appreciate not everyone will agree with me on this point and if schools have established a strategy of using KOs that they consider to be working well, then I am not suggesting changing that; if it's not broken, don't fix it!

However, after a lot of careful thought and reflection, I have developed some arguments and reasons as to why a KO should be shared with students and their families at home once all the content has been taught, rather than at the beginning of a topic.

Learning out of context – When students are provided with a KO that contains content of a whole topic, which will likely be taught over a period of time, perhaps a half or full term, they are being exposed to material that they have not yet been taught by their teacher. If students take a KO home they may attempt to learn material before the teacher has taught, discussed and addressed it in class. This can lead to students developing misconceptions as the vital teacher explanation is absent. This can also be an issue for parents and carers who try to discuss or quiz their child on content from the KO that may not have been taught at that point. Students shouldn't be quizzed on content they haven't been taught, but this could happen. Instructions can be provided on a KO or on the flip side as to when content is covered but there is limited space.

If children and their families are given the KO once all the content has been taught, the child will have developed a strong understanding of the content taught in the lesson and the parents or carers can quiz their child on any of the content as it has been taught and covered, so they should be able to answer any questions linked to the KO.

Share a KO from last term to focus on previously taught materials – Linked to the point above, I believe students should be given a KO to take home after all the content has been taught. A KO based on previously covered content can be used for revisiting and quizzing, either independently or with family members. Retrieval tasks in class can be based on previously taught content included in the KO, and students know this and can prepare for it. The topic of plants may be completed and the class moved on to another topic, but at home students are referring to the KO focusing on plants as they need to firmly commit this to long-term memory. Just because something isn't the topic of study in class anymore, it can still be the focus of retrieval quizzes.

Don't spoil the journey! – What about awe, wonder and curiosity? There may be some subjects where it is useful to share the KO during the encoding process, but this is where nuance between the different subjects must be considered. If reading and studying a story as a class, it simply wouldn't make sense to give students a KO at the beginning which would reveal elements of the plot; that would be a real spoiler!

This applies in other subjects too where we want students to learn new information as they progress through a topic. An example from my classroom is that I never gave my Year 7 students a KO on the events of 1066 until the end of the topic because I wanted to promote curiosity and engagement. I wanted my students to be asking questions throughout and be keen to find out the answers in lessons. Who would be king? Who would win at the battle? What happened next? A KO would instantly reveal that information in the first lesson for students and take away the memorable elements of engagement, surprise and storytelling.

A curiosity gap is created when there is a gap in knowledge that sparks intrigue and interest, like an itch that needs to be scratched in order to be satisfied. Teachers can create curiosity gaps in lessons, maybe by reading a story with a class and stopping at a particular point leaving the lesson on a cliffhanger. Another idea could be to ask a question or pose a problem, then reveal after lunch or the following day what the correct answer or solution is. Curiosity, awe and wonder play an important role in learning, especially at primary school and those elements can and should be planned as part of a knowledge rich curriculum.

The Vincent van Gogh knowledge organiser

A KS1 teacher shared with me a story about how they had created and provided a Van Gogh KO for their class. A few days after the KO was given to learners, a studious member of the class was very proud to demonstrate that they could recall all the facts from the KO with ease! This was impressive but the issue was that despite the confidence and correct factual recall the student wasn't able to recognise or describe any art by Van Gogh. The facts on the KO being recited seemed disconnected and isolated from his famous artwork. After this conversation I looked at various Van Gogh KOs online. They varied considerably with some mainly including examples of his artwork and minimal information, and others which were very content heavy, without examples or containing few examples of his work. Others tried to have a balance of content and art. The KO must link to the curriculum intention and aims; which could be from an art perspective or could be a wider curriculum focus linking art with history, religious education, geography, PSHE and more. The key question the teacher should be asking is what do they want their students to understand, know or be able to do linked to Van Gogh?

A document with images of artwork by Van Gogh is a collage and collection of paintings not a KO, but a collage could be more purposeful, relevant and helpful than a KO in this context. Does a KO with factual information show students what his artwork was really like or is it simply biographical? Depending on the age/year group/key stage I would argue that we want our students to have a wider contextual knowledge of the period in which Van Gogh lived and his lived experiences, as both had an impact on his artwork. However, we of course want students to be able to observe the fantastic art from the famous *Sunflowers* to *The Starry Night*, as they should be able to notice patterns with colours, styles, techniques and more.

Knowledge of Van Gogh increases a person's understanding and appreciation of his artwork, but that appreciation and awe can only be achieved through observing his artwork. Which comes first, the background knowledge and information then the art or vice versa, or should they be taught alongside each other? What is the essential knowledge about Van Gogh students should know or be able to do? Van Gogh produced almost 900 paintings and over 1000 sketches, so which paintings and sketches should be shared, focused on and discussed and why? What key vocabulary and/or key dates should be included and why? Are there any other key individuals to be included such as his brother, confidant and art dealer Theo Van Gogh or is that not essential to the study of Van Gogh in terms of the curriculum? Or is Van Gogh part of a wider study of famous artists and he is simply one key individual?

It is not for me to say what should or shouldn't be included on a Van Gogh KO, but I hope the points raised show the thoughtful nuance and careful consideration required for a KO which can support teaching and learning and still leave room for awe and wonder. And if anyone can create a sense of awe and wonder it's Van Gogh!

Knowledge organisers with different ages

I was surprised to find a range of KOs for EYFS online as there was a lot of content and information that children of that age simply would not be able to read, access and understand. If the purpose of a KO with EYFS is to support teacher planning and/or to be shared with parents and carers, that is clearly different and can be purposeful and helpful. If creating a KO for families to be able to support their child with development and learning it can be useful to provide QR codes that can be scanned and will direct parents and carers to useful websites and videos. QR codes can be created quickly, easily and at no cost online.

Coley Primary School and Nursery share their KOs on their school website for parents and carers to download and refer to. Their website states, 'We follow the EYFS curriculum and so much of the curriculum is covered by the children making their own choices within the learning environment we have created. We also have various topics which we cover each term and we have put those up below for you to see. This way if you want to learn alongside us, or would like to encourage your child to speak about some of the experiences they may be having, then reading our Knowledge Organisers is a really good place to start.'[47]

If a KO is being created to share with students, it should focus on key vocabulary with relevant supporting images and illustrations. A KO can be used with EYFS to support learners in class, as a visual resource to refer to and support home learning, but a key feature of a KO is to promote self-testing and this is not suitable or possible with EYFS students.

The way a KO is used with EYFS (if at all) will significantly vary from other KOs across all other key stages because of the age and ability of the learners. A secondary resource shouldn't be forced or shoehorned to apply to EYFS and no one realises this more than an EYFS specialist. A KO can contribute to the development of communication and language but it will have limitations with EYFS in the same way that extended written feedback is pointless at EYFS if students can't read it.

Retrieval practice plays such a central role with EYFS especially with literacy, mathematics and understanding the world, but it is a unique and special key stage and period in the development of a child. I don't think a KO is age appropriate in this context. Another reason is that many subjects are combined as part of understanding the world around us and the format and structure of a KO doesn't lend itself well to this unique EYFS framework and curriculum.

During the early years of child development and learning, verbal recall will play a key role, more so than any other key stage as children have not yet developed their reading and writing skills to a point where they

---

47   Coley Primary School (2022). *Knowledge Organisers*. Available at: https://www.coleyprimary.reading.sch.uk/nursery-knowledge-organisers/

can read and respond to questions. I believe KS1 is the ideal and most appropriate phase to introduce KOs to students and their families.

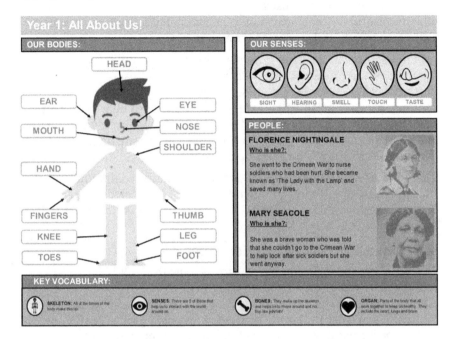

I have seen a wide range of examples from KS1, as shown above with another example created by Adam Woodward. I believe Year 1 students can start to learn what a KO is and use it as a resource to support their learning both inside and outside of the classroom. KS2 can then build on that and add more information, concepts, content, vocabulary and so on.

Knowledge organisers across different subjects

All subjects have key vocabulary that students must learn, so that aspect of a KO is applicable to every subject. There will be a range of differences across subjects in terms of content and possibly layout and structure. Every subject can also benefit from chunking information into manageable categories and sections.

Humanities subjects lend themselves very well to a KO, as history for example can include key dates, key events, key individuals as well as timelines. Geography can include maps, flags, buildings, and diagrams in addition to key information, concepts and terminology. In the study of

RE, religious symbols and artefacts can be included as well as key texts and individuals. From viewing a wide range of RE KOs the examples that were clear and concise focused on one religion rather than two or more, which is useful for comparing and contrasting but I would suggest doing that as a separate task and not to overcomplicate a KO.

An English KO can focus on grammar and punctuation, but this will cover rules and processes that students then need to apply to their written work. Keywords that students need to learn in terms of spelling, pronunciation and meaning can be included on a KO. When studying a text or story a KO can include key characters, events, themes and elements of the plot but this then links back to my point about avoiding sharing a KO too early, spoiler alert!

There has been debate online and among the maths community about the suitability of a KO in this subject, but a KO can include shapes, diagrams, explanations, examples and much more that is relevant. Once again, the crux is how a KO is used.

How to use a KO for retrieval practice in class

Following my conversation with Adam Woodward I felt inspired to create a 'knowledge organiser quizzing mat'. Adam explained that all KOs have the same structure and layout, so I created a generic humanities KO mat that could be used across year groups to promote and support class questioning, self-testing, peer quizzing and also be used at home to support parents and carers with questioning.

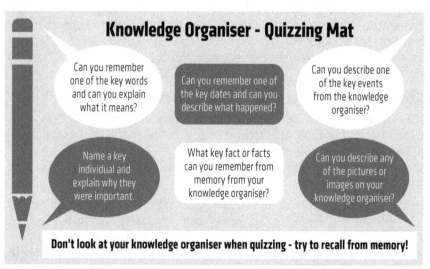

Knowledge Organiser - Quizzing Mat

Can you remember one of the key words and can you explain what it means?

Can you remember one of the key dates and can you describe what happened?

Can you describe one of the key events from the knowledge organiser?

Name a key individual and explain why they were important.

What key fact or facts can you remember from memory from your knowledge organiser?

Can you describe any of the pictures or images on your knowledge organiser?

Don't look at your knowledge organiser when quizzing - try to recall from memory!

This mat can easily be adapted with fewer or more questions and different phrasing for different subjects and topics. It can be used for verbal or written retrieval practice.

Another simple yet effective task is to ask students to recall from memory what they can about previously taught material. They write the information they can recall in the first column (this is free recall and is discussed in chapter 7). A time can be set, but if you are expecting students to write using full sentences and focus on literacy skills, then make sure adequate time is provided. For example, two minutes is too brief and students will rush, but four or five minutes is sufficient for them to recall and write key information.

The second part of the task will be for them to look at their KO (which should not have been visible during the recall stage). They can first use the KO to check if the information they have recalled is accurate and self-assess. Students can then use their KO to include additional information and content in the second column that they did not include during their recall. The template below can be used, or it can be as simple as drawing a line down a page to create two columns.

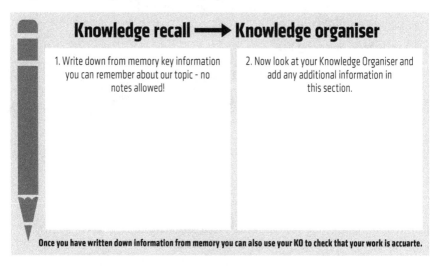

Knowledge recall ➡ Knowledge organiser

1. Write down from memory key information you can remember about our topic - no notes allowed!	2. Now look at your Knowledge Organiser and add any additional information in this section.

Once you have written down information from memory you can also use your KO to check that your work is accuarte.

A popular activity that has been shared in my previous books is 'cops and robbers'. This is very simple; students have a set amount of time to write what they can recall in the 'Cop' column. The next part of the task is to talk to their partner or peers and find additional information to steal and include in the 'Robbers' column. An addition I have made is to add a third column, where students can add even more information from their KO. This is similar to a retrieval task US teacher Blake Harvard does called 'brain – buddy – book'. Brain refers to the individual recall. Buddy involves collecting information from peers. Book then allows the students to look at their notes or textbooks to check information for accuracy and add more detail.

Cops	Robbers	Knowledge Organiser

Keep KOs and quizzes in a shared area for teachers that teach different year groups so they can refer to and use them with their classes when revisiting prior learning.

Fill in the blanks on the KO

Knowledge Organiser - Plants		
Parts of a plant	**Life Cycle of a plant**	**What do plants need to grow?**
		1. Water
		2.
		3.
		4.
		5.
Vocabulary: Roots _____	_____ - Make food for the plant using carbon dioxide from the air and sunlight.	_____ Nutrients

The example above has a lot of blanks, it would be better to focus on different sections at a time, but the example is useful for showing different ways a KO can be used with this technique. The *Parts of a plant* section has an image and boxes to illustrate which parts need labelling, this is where the learner has to recall from memory the different parts of the plant and the correct location. To differentiate this the first letter can be provided as a clue or to make it more challenging the lines and arrows can be removed.

The *Life cycle of a plant* section is completely blank, therefore this task requires much more effortful thinking and recall. If doing this type of retrieval task I would advise to do so towards the end of a topic, after lots of previous retrieval opportunities, so both retrieval strength and confidence is high.

The question about what plants need to grow, again is easy to differentiate by adding or removing clues. Students could fill this in then elaborate further with discussion in pairs. The vocabulary section would likely include more terminology, depending on the year group and level of difficulty but the focus shouldn't just be on vocabulary or definitions; students need to be able to recognise and recall key terms as well as be able to confidently and correctly explain the meaning.

If a KO is made in PowerPoint, Keynote or Google Slides it can be duplicated which will make it easy and quick to remove different sections of the KO for 'fill in the blanks' tasks (low effort, high impact).

Advice and tips

Don't include vocabulary without the definition, this is something I have observed frequently. A list of words can be given to students if the focus is spellings but it is vital students understand their meanings so they are able to use that vocabulary correctly and confidently in their written answers and verbal responses. If they are to be used at home, subject specific vocabulary could be unfamiliar to some parents and carers, but if definitions are provided this can reduce the reluctance of families to engage with the KO.

Including definitions and meaning also supports students with the application and transfer of key terms. Quigley warns, 'The rise of "knowledge organisers", and similar tools, offer opportunities to identify key vocabulary, but we should be wary of assuming stacking vocabulary in a list for some quick quizzing offers anything like the deep understanding and rich connections pupils need to make between words, phrases, concepts and big ideas.'[48]

---

48   Quigley, A. (2021). Three pillars of vocabulary teaching. *The confident teacher*. Available at: https://www.theconfidentteacher.com/2021/05/three-pillars-of-vocabulary-teaching/

Generally a KO is printed on A4 size but A3 can help students, especially those with reading difficulties or visual impairment; a lot of text on an A4 page could be challenging to read, but be more accessible if presented on A3. Some students with SEND may also find a detailed KO overwhelming so printing on A3 can support with this or the KO can be broken down and provided in sections.

If KOs are used across different subjects and topics at the same time they can be grouped together with a KO booklet to be used at home, for example, a termly KO booklet or folder.

Don't differentiate the KO. Because it contains essential knowledge, it requires all learners in the class to learn it and be able to recall it correctly. However, support and challenge can be provided to ensure all learners are able to access the knowledge on the organiser and retrieve it successfully. Imagine the workload implications if a KO was different for different learners in the classroom. This is a bad idea and goes against the key concept of all students being able to access and recall core content.

Students cannot refer to their KO during a retrieval task, even if they are struggling they must not look to a KO for the answers. It is important for students to try and challenge themselves but then use the KO to identify gaps in their knowledge and use it to close that knowledge gap.

Share the KO with ongoing enthusiasm; they can and should be used by the teacher, learner and parents and carers at home.

Further recommended reading

Making Every Primary Lesson Count: Six principles to support great teaching and learning (Making Every Lesson Count Series). Jo Payne. (2017)

Connect the Dots: The Collective Power of Relationships, Memory and Mindset in the classroom. Tricia Taylor. (2019)

Teaching WalkThrus: Visual Step-by-Step Guides to Essential Teaching Techniques. Tom Sherrington and Oliver Caviglioli. (2020)

Teach Like a Champion. 3.0 63 Techniques that Put Students on the Path to College. Doug Lemov. (2021)

CHAPTER 4
MULTIPLE CHOICE AND SHORT ANSWER QUESTIONS

Multiple choice questions (MCQs) and short answer questions (questions that require single word or short phrase or sentence answers, known as 'open response' questions in the US) feature in my previous books but not to the extent that I have dedicated a chapter to them. There are pros and cons to both multiple choice and short answer questions that are worth exploring, and evidence and tips about question design and delivery, all of which should prove useful.

Writing and designing MCQs is not as easy as it initially seems. However, that being said, I do not wish to over complicate MCQs in the classroom. I will share summaries and explanations of the evidence from research about MCQs and short answer questions and offer advice from my own classroom experiences and reflections. Writing short answer questions is ultimately easier because there is no need for the teacher to create and provide distractors as options to increase the level of challenge for students.

If you are already using MCQs in your classroom, I hope there is guidance in this chapter to help you reflect, refine and continue to use them effectively. If you are not using MCQs or only do so occasionally, I hope this chapter will encourage you to make them a regular part of your classroom routine for retrieval practice. Short answer questions can be used as an additional retrieval technique or used after MCQs as a method of removing retrieval cues.

Some educators don't use MCQs or can be reluctant to because there are potential pitfalls and problems with this technique. The main criticism is that students can resort to guessing or can simply be lucky! Evidence Based Education (EBE) is an organisation that delivers educational training and provides a wide range of resources and blogs for teachers to access. One specific blog post on the EBE website focuses on the effective use of MCQs. Ourania Ventista from EBE writes:

It is significantly unlikely that a student will get many questions correct just through pure luck. For example, in a multiple choice assessment with questions which have four alternatives, it is plausible that a student will get one or two questions right by pure luck.

Number of questions	Possibility of getting the question(s) right by 'pure' luck
1	25%
2	6%
3	1.6%
4	0.4%
5	0.09%

However, as the number of multiple choice questions increases, the possibility of a student getting a high mark by pure luck alone decreases. These possibilities do not apply though, if the student has partial knowledge. Partial knowledge helps the student to possibly exclude some of the alternatives. Nevertheless, when referring to just luck, it is unlikely that guessing can significantly distort the overall results of a test longer than 20 questions.[49]

There is the potential to simply guess but if the student knows options B and C are incorrect based on their knowledge then they have used the act of recalling information from memory to reach the right answer through informed power of elimination. Retrieval has still taken place to reach the correct answer.

Despite the limitations, I am an advocate for using MCQs in the primary classroom as there are many benefits for both teachers and students. Firstly, for the teacher a MCQ quiz can be carried out in a short amount of time within the lesson meaning that retrieval practice can still be meaningful and helpful while also enabling time for new content to be taught (not feeling that retrieval practice has unintentionally hijacked a lesson plan). This can also mean you are able to ask a greater number of questions to quiz a wider range of knowledge.

MCQs can be used to check for understanding of recently covered content, including what has been taught in the lesson (this is not

---

49   Ventista, O. (2017). *Time to increase the quality of the multiple-choice questions you use!* Evidence Based Education. Available at: https://evidencebased.education/increase-quality-multiple-choice/

retrieval practice if no forgetting has occurred because students are not recalling information from their long-term memory). MCQs can be used for retrieval practice, including key content, dates, individuals, vocabulary and more. MCQs can be versatile in terms of the content and type of questions asked which can range from factual recall to higher order thinking, if the questions are carefully crafted.

Ventista also writes about the positive aspects of teachers using MCQs:

> *First, multiple choice questions are objectively scored. In other tests, like essays, there can be disagreement between the people marking the test (raters), which can increase the measurement error and lead to low inter-rater reliability. Moreover, a multiple choice question does not take much time to answer and, therefore, a student can answer many multiple choice questions in the same time that (s)he could reply to a few open-ended questions or a single essay (Zimmaro, 2010). This enables the assessments to include more questions on the topic. Consequently, there is a broader coverage of the examined subject and therefore more representative results about the knowledge of the student (Burton et al., 1991). Furthermore, multiple choice questions are not time-consuming to mark, and finally, they can focus on a specific topic. This narrower focus can help teachers identify a specific misconception based on an alternative that a student chose. To summarise, multiple choice assessments can facilitate learning and inform reliable and valid judgments.*[50]

MCQs, when designed carefully, can address potential misconceptions or misunderstandings that may have developed in previous lessons, which is useful for the teacher to be aware of, and can support responsive teaching and future planning. MCQs can be used for both formative and summative assessment so are very versatile, but it should be clearly communicated to students when MCQs are being used for low stakes retrieval practice or for formal summative assessment.

Another benefit for the teacher is that MCQs can be very workload friendly. In terms of marking and feedback, it is not necessary for the teacher to do this (although it is important for the teacher to be monitoring and have an awareness of students' ability to recall information as well as gaps in knowledge). A MCQ quiz can be self-assessed or peer-assessed with the teacher going through the answers

---

50   Ventista, O. (2017). *Time to increase the quality of the multiple-choice questions you use!* Evidence Based Education. Available at: https://evidencebased.education/increase-quality-multiple-choice/

to discuss any misconceptions or mistakes with students. They are graded and scored objectively; answers are either right or wrong, with no need for moderation or review, hence lending themselves to self-assessment. If there is more than one teacher per year group, quizzes can easily be shared, again great for supporting workload and also consistency as all students across classes should be able to answer the same key questions to recall target memories.

If using technology, with online quizzing tools such as Kahoot or Quizizz (more information later in this chapter on technology for MCQs) they will often do the work for the teacher by instantly marking quizzes and providing immediate feedback to everyone in the class. Online quizzes also have features which enable teachers to 'teleport' questions from other public quizzes created by other teachers and use them as they are or adapt them slightly if needed. Technology has enabled teachers to create a quiz for their class with ease and speed!

Many students enjoy the act of quizzing; it is rewarding, satisfying, challenging and fun. A MCQ quiz provides students with retrieval cues, clues and a chance of getting the answer right. They can provide retrieval support for younger students and students with learning difficulties or English as an additional language (EAL), making retrieval practice accessible and inclusive, and can be differentiated through question design. MCQs can lead to opportunities for retrieval success, which can increase motivation and confidence for learners.

Question design with MCQs

Each multiple choice should contain a stem; the question. The key refers to the correct answer and distractors are the other options included. The biggest challenge when writing effective MCQs is to include relevant and plausible distractors. Research has shown that one correct answer and two plausible distractors is the optimum ratio.[51] Including more options does increase the challenge but it also increases the challenge for the teacher to include plausible distractors.

The research about MCQs suggests that this is a retrieval strategy that should be used with younger children (as discussed in chapter 1). Although a MCQ provides the answer alongside alternatives, meaning

---

51   Shank, P. (2021). *Write better multiple-choice questions to assess learning: measure what matters. Evidence-informed tactics for multiple-choice questions.* Independently published. Page 7.

the student has to recognise, identify and select a response rather than recall it from memory, this is still a retrieval task. For example, if a student is answering the question below before they had seen the options provided, they might not have known the answer.

Q. What is the capital of Kenya?

When the correct answer and plausible distractors are included, this gives the student support with a retrieval cue. The options below are plausible distractors as they are both capital cities but the level of challenge will depend on students' prior knowledge of other countries and capital cities.

Q. What is the capital of Kenya? A) Paris B) Nairobi C) Madrid

Context is key when considering challenge. For example, in my previous school in Abu Dhabi if I asked Year 5 students to name the seven emirates of the United Arab Emirates that would be an easy question for the class. It is likely most if not all students could recall all the emirates because of the environment they live in. Can you name the seven emirates?[52] Hence what may seem easy to one person can be challenging to another, it is the teacher of the class who will know where the appropriate level of challenge lies.

It is important to create MCQs that do provide a degree of challenge because the style of question itself already offers support by presenting the student with the correct answer in front of them, albeit alongside incorrect options. This again links to desirable difficulties, and the Goldilocks principle of getting it just right (not too easy or too difficult) applies. If it is a question or task too easy or too hard then little will be learned.

Dr Andrew C. Butler is an associate professor in the Department of Education and the Department of Psychological and Brain Sciences at Washington University in St. Louis. Butler has carried out and published research about multiple choice questions, and has advised that, 'The

---

52   Ajman, Abu Dhabi, Dubai, Sharjah, Fujairah, Ras Al Khaimah and Umm Al Quwain.

ideal difficulty level is a bit higher than the midpoint between chance and perfect performance.'[53]

Examples of questions with one correct answer and two plausible distractors:

This KS1 maths question has 50 as the correct answer but if a student selects 15 they have added the numbers together instead of using multiplication and if a student selects 500 they have added an extra 0 and multiplied by 100. The example below also has one clear answer and two plausible distractors.

Q) What building did Guy Fawkes and the people he worked with try to blow up?

   A) Buckingham Palace

   B) Houses of Parliament

   C) Westminster Abbey

This example is slightly different, the two incorrect answers are simply other well known buildings in London. However, students may select Buckingham Palace if they know Guy Fawkes and his conspirators were aiming to kill the king and that is where the royal family live. Students could select Westminster Abbey if they recall that religion was a motivating factor behind the plot. Answering this question incorrectly could simply show a lack of knowledge and/or ability to recall the correct information, or it could help to identify where a student has specifically gone wrong, like the maths example above.

The examples above are also presented in the same format; vertically in contrast to horizontal and using letters in contrast to numbers. This provides a clear and consistent layout. Using letters instead of numbers can help avoid confusion, especially with maths questions or

---

53   Butler, A. C. (2018). Multiple-choice testing in education: Are the best practices for assessment also good for learning? *Journal of Applied Research in Memory and Cognition*, 7(3), 323–331.

any options that include numbers such as dates, figures and statistics. Both the examples above can be used as short answer questions with students writing their responses on a mini whiteboard, in their exercise books, digitally or on an exit ticket. The key difference is that a MCQ provides more retrieval support with cued recall in contrast to free recall, and as discussed in chapter 1, younger learners do initially need retrieval cues and support.

Avoid using complex question styles or answer formats. Complexity with retrieval practice can cause confusion, misunderstanding and students can resort to guesswork instead of recall. A key theme with question design in this chapter is simplicity. Simple in terms of the phrasing and layout of the question so that MCQs are genuinely providing opportunities for retrieval practice. Consider the language and terminology used, linking to the point above. Unless the question is focusing on vocabulary it is advisable to use tier two vocabulary rather than tier three so all students can understand what the question is actually asking.

Design and ask questions that require precise recall. Ensure that questions focus on the specific aspects of knowledge, concepts, content or thought processes that you want to assess. This was discussed in chapter 2 with curriculum design; focusing on the core content and essential knowledge in contrast to generalised trivia. Avoid opinion-based questions or where there is the possibility of debate, MCQs are not the right platform for it as shown below:

Q. Which of the following books by Roald Dahl is the most popular?
A) Matilda
B) George's Marvellous Medicine
C) Charlie and the Chocolate Factory
D) Other

This could be an interesting and thought-provoking discussion or debate in pairs, groups or among the class, with students arguing their case for which book is best or most popular and why, but it is not appropriate for a MCQ. It is opinion-based and there are so many variables to consider. Popular is difficult to define, does it refer to popular within the class or overall sales or in reference to film or theatre shows? There are simply some topics, tasks and questions that don't lend themselves to MCQs and some that do.

Patti Shank PHD authored a book specifically dedicated to MCQs entitled *Write Better Multiple-Choice Questions to Assess Learning*. I found it an interesting read, but the intended audience was not solely teachers and educators, with a lot of advice directed at companies and organisations as to how they can use MCQs with adults. Despite this, there were evidence-informed suggestions and many references to research provided. I would recommend this book if perhaps you are considering an action research project or assignment on MCQs for a qualification, but bear in mind that it is not written specifically for teachers.

Shank makes a lot of valid points, writing that, 'Everyone who uses multiple choice questions must be able to write them so participants aren't frustrated and can show what they learned.'[54] This is an important point for teachers to consider about the ability to write and design MCQs so they are accessible. We want to challenge students; sometimes challenges can be frustrating but MCQs require a balance of retrieval difficulty and retrieval success.

Shank has noted that, 'Research is clear that well written multiple choice questions can measure a wide range of important learning outcomes, including analysis, decision making and problem solving.'[55] This chapter focuses on using MCQs and short answer questions for retrieval practice, a learning strategy not an assessment strategy. Shank writes, 'The primary goal is to examine what participants struggle with and what does not work well, then to fix those issues.'[56] This is ultimately responsive teaching and while I would argue that the primary goal of MCQs for retrieval practice is to enhance and boost long-term memory and recall, identifying areas of strength and gaps in knowledge is very helpful for both the teacher and student.

I advise teachers to only include one correct answer, because where there is more than one correct answer this can add further pressure and lead to confusion. If students select one correct and incorrect option, at a later date they can confuse which of those were correct and which was incorrect (I share this from experience). Including two correct answers can be used as a strategy with older students in secondary, but I think should be avoided with primary students. Keeping the focus

---

54   Shank, P. (2021). *Write better multiple-choice questions to assess learning: measure what matters. Evidence-informed tactics for multiple-choice questions*. Independently published. Page 4.

55   Ibid. Page 9.

56   Ibid. Page 10.

on one correct answer is clearer, simpler and more memorable. Adding more than one correct answer will also lead to adding more options and distractors, more time will be needed to answer the question and if a student selects two incorrect answers that can be a double layer of disappointment.

For example this question is about key themes in the play *Romeo and Juliet* and there are multiple correct answers.

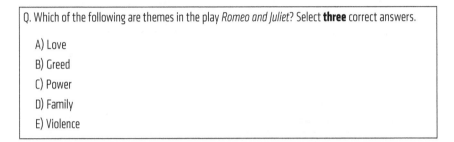

Shank offers this advice, 'Good distractors should be plausible to people who do not know the content being tested.'[57] This resonated with me, because as part of my research for the book *Retrieval Practice 2: Implementing, Embedding and Reflecting* I did number of online quizzes. I purposefully completed quizzes where I had limited or no knowledge of a topic, yet despite my lack of knowledge I was still able to score very highly. The reason for this was not lucky guesses or underestimating my own abilities, but instead poor question design, especially with distractors which were often not plausible.

Steven J. Burton and his colleagues published *How to Prepare Better Multiple-Choice Test Items: Guidelines for University Faculty* in 1991. Burton provided this advice to create plausible distractors, 'Use common student misconceptions as distractors. The incorrect answers supplied by students to a short answer version of the same item are a good source of material to use in constructing distractors for a multiple-choice item. Develop your own distractors, using words that "ring a bell" or that "sound official". Your distractors should be plausible enough to keep the student who has not achieved the objective from detecting them, but not so subtle that they mislead the student who

57   Shank, P. (2021). *Write better multiple-choice questions to assess learning: measure what matters. Evidence-informed tactics for multiple-choice questions.* Independently published. Page 57.

has achieved the objective.'[58] Keep the level of depth for each distractor option the same, for example all one word or all extended sentences. More depth for the correct answer can be a giveaway!

Include the option 'I don't know yet'

Including the option 'I don't know yet' links in with the growth mindset approach of not knowing... yet. It also encourages students to be honest and avoid guessing. This will be more insightful for the teacher in comparison to trying to figure out if a student was able to recall the correct answer, had an educated guess or simply a lucky guess. Students may think this is pointless and they would rather guess than select this option but that is why it's important to explain that identifying gaps in knowledge so those gaps can be closed is helpful for learning.

This option also supports a low stakes approach, but we do want students to attempt to answer questions and not go for the easy opt out option. The ways I have used this with my classes vary. At times I have only included this option with difficult questions. Another way is to say students are not allowed to use this option more than three times (this amount can vary depending on how many questions are asked). This ensures students think carefully about when to use this option as they cannot rely on it for every question. During a conversation with *Teach Like a Champion* author Doug Lemov, I asked what his thoughts were on including 'I don't know yet'. He suggested an alternative to 'I don't know yet', which involved including an option on MCQs for students who aren't sure but with language that asks them to practice recalling what they do know. So 'I don't know yet...' could become 'I know that ...'.

Lemov and I co-authored a blog on hybrid question design and we wrote that choosing the option to add what students can recall – although it isn't the answer to the question but is relevant – isn't a shortcut for students who seek to avoid full effort. We liked the idea of adding a choice that reads, 'I know that...' with students then asked to fill in the blank describing as much as they could recall on the topic, as shown below.[59]

---

58   Burton, S. J., Sudweeks, R. R., Merrill, P. F. and Wood, B. (1991). *How to Prepare Better Multiple-Choice Test Items: Guidelines for University Faculty*. Provo, UT: Brigham Young University Testing Services and The Department of Instructional Science.

59   Lemov, D. and Jones, K. (2021). On hybrid question design in retrieval practice – with Kate Jones. *Teach Like a Champion*. Available at: https://teachlikeachampion.com/blog/on-hybrid-question-design-in-retrieval-practice-with-kate-jones/

Q. Who killed Archduke Franz Ferdinand in 1914?

A) Kaiser Wilhelm

B) Gavrilo Princip

C) Nedjelko Cabrinovic

D) I know that...

A student might not be able to recall the name of the assassin (Gavrilo Princip) but they could write 'I know that the death of Franz Ferdinand in 1914 was a cause of WW1'. Lemov and I discussed taking this style of question further by combining MCQs and free recall, as shown below.

Q1. Who killed Archduke Franz Ferdinand in 1914?

A) Kaiser Wilhelm

B) Gavrilo Princip

C) Nedjelko Cabrinovic

D) I know that...

Q2. How did this lead to the outbreak of WW1?

This is combining elaboration with MCQs but the challenge would be the feedback. MCQs can be self-assessed and checked with teacher guidance in the lesson, sharing and discussing answers. For free recall answers it is worth the teacher skimming and scanning responses to check for accurate recall.

There are other ways to add opportunities for elaboration with MCQs. I was teaching a Year 4 class that were completing a MCQ quiz on paper and highlighting the answers they deemed correct. As I was walking around the class during this task, lots of students wanted to recall and share extra information with me. Their enthusiasm to recall further information inspired me to create the resource below where students have the opportunity to elaborate if they can, but it is not compulsory, rather it is an optional challenge to stretch students. My students responded well to this and as we discussed the answers as a class, where students self-assessed their answers, there were also opportunities for students to share with each other their extended points linked to the question.

Multiple Choice Question	Elaboration
Read the question carefully, then highlight what you think is the correct answer.	Do you know anything else you can add that is linked to this question? Any further information can be included in this column.
Q1) What year did WW2 begin? a) 1914 b) 1939 c) 1945 d) I don't know yet	WW2 started in 1939 and lasted six years because it ended in 1945. In 1945 people celebrated VE day in the UK with lots of parties and celebrations in the streets.
Q2) Who was the Prime Minister during WW2? a) David Lloyd George b) Stanley Baldwin c) Winston Churchill d) I don't know yet	
Q3) Which city did evacuees come from that stayed in our local area? a) Liverpool b) Manchester c) Cardiff d) I don't know yet	Children were evacuated from big cities because they were dangerous and more likely to be bombed. They left to be safe and the Welsh countryside was a safe place for evacuees to go and families would look after them until the war ended.

In the questions above there is a correct answer and two plausible distractors. I have seen lots of MCQs where at least one is a comedy option (I refer to this as 'The Bradley Walsh effect' because this is commonly used on the popular television quiz show The Chase!). I once saw Lady Gaga as an option asking which of the following was married to Henry VIII. Adding Boris Johnson as an option for the question about the Prime Minister in WW2 might provide a giggle but it does dilute the level of challenge and recall.

There are also times where a comedy answer isn't suitable, for example in sensitive topics such as the Holocaust, PSHE and so on. Burton comments on this, observing, 'Unrealistic or humorous distractors are nonfunctional and increase the student's chance of guessing the correct answer.'[60]

If you and your classes absolutely love a comedy option my advice is to make it an exception, so not with every question and perhaps keep two plausible distractors to keep the challenge while keeping the comedy element. There are students who select the comedy option, although they know it is incorrect, in an attempt to be funny. Teachers can't penalise students for selecting the comedy option as it was there as an option for them to select, so when trying to include humour use it with caution and try to find other opportunities to bring it into the classroom.

Another option, similar to the one above as it allows for elaboration, is to ask students to explain how they know the answer is correct. This is shown in the example below.

Multiple Choice Question	Explanation
Read the question carefully, then highlight what you think is the correct answer.	Explain or show why you think this answer is correct. You can include your working out in this column.
Q1) 2 x 8 = a) 6 b) 10 c) 16 d) I don't know yet	
Q2) 75 X 5 = a) 80 b) 150 c) 375 d) I don't know yet	75 x 5 ——— 375
Q3) 64 X 100 = a) 64 b) 640 c) 6400 d) I don't know yet	Add an extra 0 when x by 100.

60   Burton, S. J., Sudweeks, R. R., Merrill, P. F. and Wood, B. (1991). *How to Prepare Better Multiple-Choice Test Items: Guidelines for University Faculty*. Provo, UT: Brigham Young University Testing Services and The Department of Instructional Science.

The example on the previous page has shown very clearly how the student has been able to reach the correct answer for the second question and where they have gone wrong for the third question. Again, this can be used with short answer questions too.

Short Answer Question	Elaboration
Read the question carefully and write your answer underneath.	Do you know anything else you can add that is linked to this question? Any further information can be included in this column.
Q1) What year did WW2 begin? 1939	WW2 started in 1939 and lasted six years because it ended in 1945. In 1945 people celebrated VE day in the UK with lots of parties and celebrations in the streets.
Q2) Who was the Prime Minister during WW2? Winston Churchill And/or Neville Chamberlain	
Q3) Which city did evacuees come from that stayed in our local area? Liverpool	Children were evacuated from big cities because they were dangerous and more likely to be bombed. They left to be safe and the Welsh countryside was a safe place for evacuees to go and families would look after them until the war ended.

Avoid 'All' or 'None of the above' with MCQs

I have found that engaging with evidence from research can do the following:

1. Confirm what I am already doing in my classroom.
2. Inform my knowledge and understanding of how children learn.
3. Challenge my current classroom practice.

I can recall reading the work of Butler where he suggested that 'all of the above' and 'none of the above' should be avoided in MCQ quizzes. This surprised me as it is something I have done a lot in the past without considering the possible issues. The paper from Butler did challenge my classroom practice and made me reflect on the use and purpose of using 'all' and 'none of the above' with MCQs. I thought this strategy would check if students were reading the questions and answers carefully but then this might appear as though we are trying to trick or catch them out.

I believed providing the option 'all of the above' worked well when there were a range of correct answers to a question. The issue with 'all of the above' is how do we mark this? If a student selects an option that isn't 'all of the above', this will be classed as incorrect when in fact it is a correct answer, it's just not the one the teacher was looking for. This can cause confusion that we should try to avoid.

Example 1

Q1) Which of the following was a contender to the throne in 1066?

A) Harold Godwinson

B) Harald Hardrada

C) William Duke of Normandy

D) All of the above

The problem with the example above is that the correct answer is D, but if a student selects A, B or C they are also correct. If I were to tell my student option A is correct as are the others, they may later recall that Harold Godwinson was a contender and that the others were incorrect. A is not incorrect in terms of the content of the question but it fails to show that B and C were correct also. It's complicated and problematic. There could instead be a range of questions, which emphasise that all three were contenders to the throne:

Example 2

Q2) Which of the contenders to the throne in 1066 was from England?

A) Harold Godwinson

B) Harald Hardrada

C) William Duke of Normandy

This question mentions that all the individuals were contenders but asks students to recall which specific contender was English (Harold Godwinson) and knowing where the contenders were from is essential knowledge.

I think 'none of the above' is pointless, although I am aware others disagree with me on this. The review by Butler explains that the issue with this approach is that if the correct option is 'none of the above' time has been wasted as students have been exposed to a range of incorrect answers, so what actually was the point of the question? Students should be retrieving and selecting the correct answer and this type of question takes that opportunity away from them. A wasted retrieval opportunity.

Example 3

> Q3) Which religion celebrates Passover?
>
> A) Buddhism
> B) Islam
> C) Sikhism
> D) None of the above

This is quite an obvious problem, yet 'none of the above' is often used in MCQ quizzes. A student may select option D and they would be correct, but do they know the religion is Judaism? We can't tell or explicitly infer that from their response therefore the information it provides is limited and students have only been exposed to incorrect answers. It can also be frustrating for the student that does know the religion is Judaism but does not have the opportunity to select that or show that knowledge. A student may assume the correct answer is Christianity as it is a world religion they are aware of that is not included, hence the possibility of confusion and error.

Case study: Multiple choice questions in mathematics by Neil Almond and Shannen Doherty.

Maths takes place every day in the primary classroom, therefore retrieval practice with maths should be taking place daily too. I have followed the work of Shannen Doherty and Neil Almond, learning a lot from them both as I consider them to be two of the leading experts in primary maths. Shannen and Neil are two evidence-informed teachers who have supported other teachers through their writing and sharing. Shannen and Neil have collaborated for this case study to offer their expertise and advice about retrieval practice in maths.

The primary mathematics curriculum is vast. The amount of content that we ask ten- and eleven-year-olds to master by the end of Year 6 can quickly overwhelm our students. This can then lead to the development of a negative mindset towards the subject of mathematics; potentially putting them off it for life.

While it is true that the mathematics curriculum places strong demands on the number of ideas and concepts that are to be learned, we can use the very nature of mathematics, its hierarchical structure, to our advantage to support students in their mathematical journey. Learning mathematics is not a linear experience, for the ideas and concepts that are written into the curriculum get repeated as students progress through school. With a solid knowledge of those repeating concepts, ideas and the connections between them, along with a deep understanding of the role retrieval practice has on the learning process, it is possible for most students to feel successful in primary mathematics.

One classroom strategy that can be used from the principle of retrieval practice is that of multiple choice questions. These are powerful in their utility not only because they can bring about gains in learning by making students recall certain mathematical facts and procedures, but also through their use as a diagnostic tool to help guide teacher feedback when the incorrect answers (distractors) mirror common misconceptions. Because of this powerful, multi-purpose use, multiple choice questions make regular appearances in our maths lessons. What follows is a worked example as to how they are used.

For a recent lesson on adding and subtracting mixed numbers, the prerequisites were first identified. This is the core prior knowledge that students will need to have in their long-term memories for students to learn this next step. During the planning process, the following prerequisites were identified as being the most crucial:

■ Addition and subtraction of fractions with the same denominator.

- Partitioning.
- Common multiples.
- The equivalent nature of improper fractions and mixed numbers.
- When the numerator is equal to the denominator, this is one whole.

Once these were identified, writing high quality multiple choice questions was the next step. To guide our thinking in this step, we used the principles in Evidence Based Education's *Designing Great Assessment - the case for using multiple choice questions for accurate assessment.*

These are the principles outlined in that publication:

- Always phrase the stem as a question rather than as a statement.
- Use vertical formatting and letters for answers/distractors.
- The distractors should be similar to the key (the correct answer). Ideally, these should tap into common misconceptions and errors that are associated with the topic in hand.
- Avoid unnecessarily difficult vocabulary and grammar (unless, of course, this is what you are testing for).
- Avoid opinion-based subjective questions.
- Avoid negatively phrased stems. There is also no need for more than two distractors, especially as they can be so hard to write.

These were the multiple choice questions that were written based on those principles.

1. What is 5/8 + 2/8?

   1. 7/8
   2. 7/16
   3. 3/8

2. Which answer partitions 5.34 into the correct place value?

  1. 5 ones and 34 tenths
  2. 5 ones, 4 hundredths and 3 tenths
  3. 5 ones, 3 tenths and 4 hundredths

3. Which of these answers only contain common multiples of 6 and 9?

  1. 1, 3
  2. 18, 36, 54, 72, 90
  3. 6, 9, 12, 18, 24, 27

4. If the longer dark grey bar represents the whole, which answer represents the image below?

  1. 1, 6/6
  2. $1^{1/5}$, 6/5
  3. 2, 1/5

5. Which answer makes the mathematical statement correct?

When the numerator is _____ the denominator, this is one whole.

  1. equal to
  2. greater than
  3. less than

Those familiar with the key stage 2 mathematics curriculum will see that the content that students are asked to retrieve includes concepts of Years 3, 4 and 5. As these are designed to test the prerequisite knowledge needed for understanding the learning of adding and subtracting mixed numbers, it is crucial that these are answered before that unit is to be taught, so that any amendments to the sequence of learning can be made before moving on to the new objective.

As mentioned previously, these multiple choice questions serve a dual purpose. By asking students to answer these questions, they are engaging in retrieval practice – in this case thinking deeply about primary mathematics – to bring content from their long-term memory into their working memory. The multiple choice aspect makes it easy for the teacher to gather the data of the whole class using a range of simple techniques from mini-whiteboards to showing a number of fingers to represent one of the three options. Those who choose an incorrect answer clearly show the teacher the misconceptions the students have and corrective instruction can be applied to remedy their misunderstandings before moving on to the new content. Those who got the answer correct have successfully retrieved and activated the important prior knowledge and concepts needed to take the next steps on their mathematical journey.

By carefully selecting and retrieving mathematical content based on the prerequisite knowledge, we can ensure that most of our students are able to progress and learn the mathematical content that will enable them to become numerate and, thus, increase their chances of being successful members of their communities and society at large.

Thank you to Neil and Shannen. You can follow Neil on Twitter @Mr_AlmondEd and visit his teaching and learning blog https://nutsaboutteaching.wordpress.com/. Shannen is on Twitter @MissSDoherty and her blog is https://missdohertysthoughts.wordpress.com/. I also highly recommend 100 Ideas for Primary Teachers: Maths **authored by Shannen.**

Use of images with MCQs

Images can be used across a range of subjects and topics including science, maths, humanities, art and design, physical education and more. This is a great option for MCQs in the primary classroom. The examples below have three plausible distractors; it can be easier to add plausible distractors when using images but I would not advise more than four options, with the correct answer and three competitors.

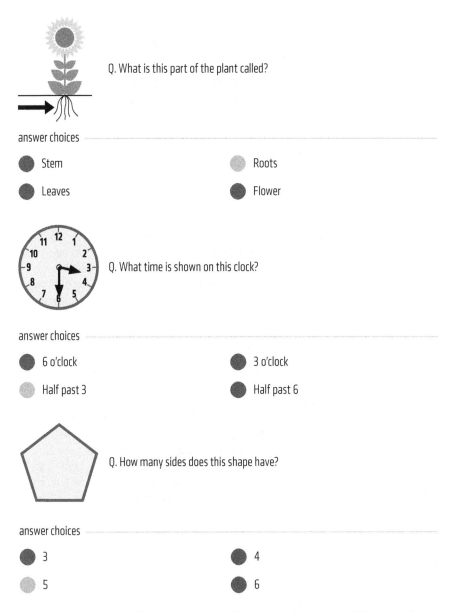

Q. What is this part of the plant called?

answer choices

● Stem   ● Roots

● Leaves   ● Flower

Q. What time is shown on this clock?

answer choices

● 6 o'clock   ● 3 o'clock

● Half past 3   ● Half past 6

Q. How many sides does this shape have?

answer choices

● 3   ● 4

● 5   ● 6

It is easy to form habits with MCQs where they become solely used for factual recall, but they can be used for higher order thinking and to support literacy across the curriculum. MCQs are great for checking for understanding and recall, and depending when they are used, to select accurate tenses, spellings, homophones and more, while short answer questions allow opportunities for students to practise spellings of key terms and basic punctuation.

Mini white boards for MCQs and short answer questions

Mini white boards (MWBs) or 'show me boards' are not a new classroom tool for supporting teaching and learning, but like any tool they can be used well or badly, effectively or ineffectively. Students must be explicitly trained how to use their MWB in a lesson. This should link with the behaviour policy otherwise it can be tempting for students to write or draw silly or inappropriate things and it can be used to distract and hinder learning instead of being a tool to check for understanding and retrieval practice.

The boards are ideal for MCQs because the amount of text on a MWB should be minimal. MCQs can be embedded into a presentation or written on the board for students to see (don't verbally ask MCQs without the question and answer options visible as this can be difficult to hold in working memory and students can easily and quickly forget the questions and the options). Students simply write down A, B or C on their MWB to show what they think is the correct answer. This makes it possible for the class teacher to see all responses and provide instant feedback as well as informing their decisions about future planning.

A common mistake I have made myself and seen during lesson observations, is allowing students to raise their boards at different points. Some students wait to see what others have written as their answer before writing. To avoid this issue of copying and cheating it's best to use the '1-2-3 show me' method. Make sure students are given sufficient thinking time to recall the answer and write the letter that represents their answer. Instruct students they are not to raise their MWB until explicitly told to do so. When the teacher says '1-2-3 show me' all MWBs are raised at the same time. The fact the MWB simply has a letter enables the teacher to scan the class to check for accuracy or address any mistakes or misconceptions.

If students don't know the answer, try to encourage them to avoid guessing and instead draw a large '?' on their MWB. This very clearly identifies gaps in knowledge that the teacher can pick up on and address with the whole class or on an individual level.

Another benefit of using a MWB for both MCQ and short answer questions is that they are incredibly low stakes, and the answers, once seen by the teacher are erased away. This is informal, no recording of scores and as well as being low stakes they are workload friendly for teachers because they provide insight without the need for written marking or feedback, as instant verbal feedback can be provided.

Teacher Matt Swain shared a routine he uses in his classroom for a more forensic approach to checking for understanding and recall using MWBs. He uses it to help stagger the data and responses coming from students and to ensure every board is checked. If your classroom is laid out using rows, instead of an all at once approach you could try one row at a time as suggested by Matt and illustrated below.

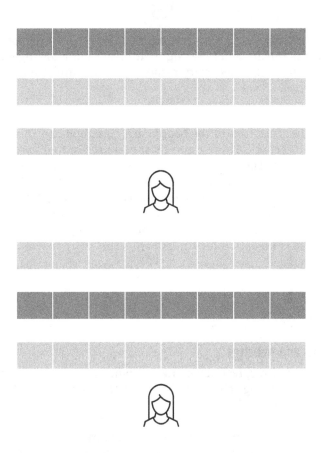

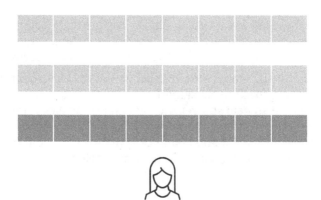

Another alternative to '1-2-3 show me' is a 'Mexican wave' approach with students raising and lowering their MWBs but allowing enough time for the teacher to see every response. Matt shared this on Twitter, @mattswain36.

MCQ cards

Not all teachers are fans of the boards in a classroom, so an alternative is to have MCQ cards. These can consist of a pack of four cards that each student has. They work best as an A5 size, with the letters A, B, and C printed clearly on each card and another with a ?. When a question is asked the students select the card with the letter they think represents the correct answer. The same principles of using MWBs apply with '1-2-3, show me'. The limitation of MCQ cards is that unlike boards, there is no option for students to write short answer responses.

Online tools and websites

Due to the pandemic, technology has become much more integral to teaching and learning. There can be frustrations with technology, both inside and outside of the classroom but we can harness the benefits of technology, especially for retrieval practice with low stakes quizzing. I regularly use technology in my lessons and after trial and error and reflections, when it comes to using technology for retrieval practice, I have five key principles that I share with teachers when considering what technology to use or not use.

1. Keep it low stakes

Does the online tool provide opportunities for low stakes quizzing or other retrieval practice tasks? In a previous school we experienced online learning for a significant amount of time as a result of the pandemic. Formal summative assessment continued but had to be completed online; across the school Google Forms was the agreed platform to use. These assessments (although completed at home, and therefore didn't have the same level of credibility and reliability as an in-school assessment) were graded and results were sent to parents and carers via reporting channels. This was very high stakes for our students. As the school decided to use Google Forms for assessments, we used alternatives apps and websites for retrieval practice to make a clear distinction between low stakes quizzing and assessments. It's important to make this very clear to students. Many websites such as Kahoot and Quizizz are low stakes in the style they are presented.

2. Ensure it is workload friendly

As mentioned previously, in order for retrieval practice to become embedded as daily practice and routine it has to be sustainable for teachers in terms of workload. Technology can support teacher workload, especially with quizzing. Quizizz.com has a 'teleport' feature, where it is possible to search through other public quizzes created and shared by teachers and take questions from their quiz and teleport them to your own. Once teleported, the question and/or the options can be edited. This enables teachers to create high quality quizzes quickly and easily (other websites have similar features). Most online quizzes instantly mark questions, providing immediate feedback to students and teachers. Some websites provide data for teachers to use to inform their planning as they will highlight where individuals or the whole class scored correctly or incorrectly.

3. Provide variety with question design

This chapter is dedicated to MCQs and short answer questions, but the following chapter explores cued and free recall. There are many websites that provide a wide range of question design, allowing the teacher to ask MCQs and short answer questions. These sites often include cued recall, with the option to provide prompts such as images, audio, or equations; and free recall, with students answering questions from memory with no prompts. It can be tempting to rely heavily on MCQs but they do have their limitations, hence the need to vary the question design.

4. Provide variety with the technology

Naturally, people have their own preferences and teachers are no different! Despite my personal preferences I make sure I don't only use one quizzing tool or website. Some teachers do, and I understand the arguments, such as embedding a platform as a classroom routine and promoting consistency, but there are so many fantastic websites and apps for retrieval practice that we shouldn't limit ourselves to just one. We certainly shouldn't use too many, as we want students to become familiar with the online tools so that using them becomes automatic to them and they can focus on the recall element. We can trial different websites and then rotate between them to provide some variety, and because there are differences between the websites, it's worth exploring which would work well in your classroom.

5. Ensure it is user friendly

Finally, and arguably most importantly, is to consider how user friendly the website or app is for both the teacher and students. Teachers need to be able to understand how to create or set a quiz, as well as review answers and ensure feedback has been provided. Students also need to understand how to access the quiz and answer the questions. If a website or app is complicated this will become the focus of working memory, taking capacity away from the act of retrieval. Most websites and apps are very user friendly but if they are proving to be a challenge ask someone for support (there are often YouTube tutorials with guidance and advice for most websites) or simply find an alternative to use.

Suggested online platforms for retrieval practice

Quizizz	Quizlet	Kahoot	Mentimeter
Flipgrid	Blooklet	Carousel Learn	Jamboard
Google Forms	Microsoft Forms	Plickers	NearPod
Socrative	Edpuzzle	Peardeck	Podsie
Math Shed	Spelling Shed	Phonics Shed	Quiz Shed
Seneca Learn	Showbie	Padlet	Anki
Show My Homework	Remember More	Apple Classroom	Diagnostic Questions

The table includes a range of online retrieval practice resources (it is important to check that the app or website is age appropriate). I will not go into the specific details in terms of instructions and pros and cons of each because there are simply too many. A lot of the websites and apps are continually evolving with new features and functions being added or removed as they improve and develop, and of course new websites and tools will also be introduced.

The key aspect is to consider the five key principles above and strike the balance between automaticity, with apps and websites being so familiar to students they become automatic in terms of using them inside the classroom, and variety, so that students don't become bored. As there is so much choice it's useful to rotate between three or four different styles of online quizzing. In addition to thinking carefully about the tool it's important to spend time on the question design too.

Feedback

It is vital that feedback is provided. Based on my own reflections I realised feedback and reflection time is something I had skimmed previously or not dedicated enough time to. The EEF published an informative guidance report entitled *Teacher Feedback to Improve Pupil Learning* and although this report goes beyond formative assessment feedback it does provide useful advice for teachers drawn from a large evidence base.

The EEF warns teachers that, 'Not all feedback has positive effects. Done badly, feedback can even harm progress. Nor is feedback "free". Large amounts of time are spent providing pupils with feedback, perhaps not always productively.'[61] Feedback provided for retrieval practice tasks should not be workload heavy for the teacher and it should be easy to understand for students. It should identify areas of recall and gaps in knowledge for both the teacher and learner. Retrieval practice should be happening on a daily basis in the primary classroom therefore it is not possible, sustainable or useful for teachers to be constantly providing lengthy feedback, which would also contradict the low stakes nature of retrieval practice.

Methods of feedback with retrieval practice include:

- **Self-assessment, self-checking and self-correcting** – This can be with ticks and crosses and can be done across subjects. It must always be supervised and led by the teacher in the classroom.

61 Collin, J. and Quigley, A. (2021). *Teacher Feedback to Improve Pupil Learning*. Education Endowment Foundation. Available at: https://educationendowmentfoundation.org.uk/education-evidence/guidance-reports/feedback

- **Peer-assessment** – This can be done with ease but for some students it can increase the stakes of the retrieval task as their partner will be marking their responses. As mentioned previously, Dylan Wiliam said 'the best person to mark a test is the person who has just taken the test'. Peer feedback should also be supervised and guided by the teacher.

- **Instant verbal feedback from the teacher** – This can be done with mini white boards as the teacher scans a class set of responses and can respond immediately.

- **Written feedback** – This is something I rarely do with retrieval practice. If students have written an extended answer I will read it and provide feedback, either verbal or written but there are a range of reasons why I rarely provide lengthy written comments. Firstly, if I provided written feedback for every member of the class that will delay the feedback process as it is not possible to do so in a lesson with X number of students. There is research published focusing on delaying feedback but with retrieval practice it helps students to have feedback sooner rather than later so they are aware of gaps in knowledge and can focus on closing those gaps. Secondly, this is not the best use of my time and it will become a workload issue. I will provide more detailed written feedback during extended writing or assessment tasks, not retrieval practice tasks.

- **Online tools or apps** – Many online quizzes will instantly mark questions, providing immediate feedback for the student and insight for the teacher.

- **Parental feedback** – This will obviously happen outside of the classroom, but it is important to ensure parents and carers understand what content to quiz their child on and how to check if the answers provided are correct or not. This is where a knowledge organiser or quizzing booklet can be very helpful.

I am confident with my MCQ quizzes and short answer question design but this has not been the case throughout my teaching career. This confidence has stemmed from engaging with research about question design, acting on the evidence, learning from other teachers who have shared examples and advice, and finally, my own reflections.

NQTs and ECTs are novice question designers, as not enough time is dedicated to question design during ITT/ITE (this is not a criticism as there is a huge amount of content to cover during this time). Question design is not often explored as part of professional development sessions, or at least it hasn't been in my experience. The concern I have for teachers early in their career is that they may search online for examples of MCQs. It is a good idea to look at what is available and this is something I still do as an experienced teacher, but quality assurance is an issue as not all resources and quizzes published online are high quality; some are but the quality varies significantly.

I would encourage experienced teachers to share resources (not just in terms of MCQs and retrieval practice tasks) and all teachers should seek feedback from others on their MCQs. The feedback could be positive and reaffirming, or there could be an error or flaw that is picked up by someone else. The same is true about students being novice question designers, so we shouldn't expect them to be able to write effective and challenging MCQs for self-testing. If we do want students to self-test, and I would only recommend this for KS2 classes, then teachers should model this explicitly with clear examples explained and discussed. Clarity and consistency should be themes throughout the question design process; and avoiding styles of questions that could potentially confuse students. Burton writes, 'Well-written multiple-choice test questions do not confuse students, and yield scores that are more appropriate to use in determining the extent to which students have achieved educational objectives.'[62]

Studies suggest avoiding the use of negatives in the stem. Burton states, 'Just because the student knows an incorrect answer does not necessarily imply that he or she knows the correct answer. For this reason, items of the negative variety are not recommended for general use.'[63] I also would advise against the use of negatives, I have rarely used this device, and when I did it was with older secondary students. Burton explains that there can be exceptions to the advice not to use negatives, but it is still worth taking caution, 'Occasionally, negative items are appropriate for objectives dealing with health or safety issues, where knowing what not to do is important. In these situations, negative items must be carefully worded to avoid confusing the student. The negative word should be placed in the stem, not in the alternatives, and should be emphasised by using underlining, italics, bold face, or CAPITALS. In addition, each of the alternatives should be phrased positively to avoid forming a confusing double negative with the

---

62   Ibid.
63   Ibid.

stem.'[64] Keep the content of the question or stem relevant and precise. Burton continues, 'Include as much of the item as possible in the stem, but do not include irrelevant material.'[65]

Further advice from Burton suggests to, 'Word the alternatives clearly and concisely. Clear wording reduces student confusion, and concise wording reduces the reading burden placed on the student.'[66] When the question or stem includes a lot of complex or lengthy words it may take the student longer to read, understand and comprehend what is being asked before they select the correct answer. Alternatively, the student may not spend long enough reading the question as they do not fully grasp it, and go on to select an incorrect option.

Multiple choice and short answer questions can be very effective in a classroom for checking for understanding, recalling information and eliciting evidence of learning. However, this efficacy will depend heavily on question design. Teachers need to think carefully about the questions they ask students and when those questions are asked in the learning process. An effectively designed question can provide the teacher with useful insight and support learners to boost their retrieval strength.

Further recommended reading

Making Good Progress? The future of Assessment for Learning. Daisy Christodoulou. (2017)

The CRAFT of Assessment: A whole school approach to assessment for learning: A whole school approach to assessment of learning. Michael Chiles. (2020)

Write better multiple-choice questions to assess learning: measure what matters – Evidence-informed tactics for multiple-choice questions. Patty Shank PHD. (2021)

Organise Ideas: Thinking by Hand, Extending the Mind. Oliver Caviglioli and David Goodwin. (2021)

---

64   Burton, S. J., Sudweeks, R. R., Merrill, P. F. and Wood, B. (1991). *How to Prepare Better Multiple-Choice Test Items: Guidelines for University Faculty.* Provo, UT: Brigham Young University Testing Services and The Department of Instructional Science.

65   Ibid.

66   Ibid.

CHAPTER 5
RETRIEVAL CUES AND FREE RECALL

Retrieval cues to support learning

We all encounter retrieval cues on a daily basis in many forms. A smell can remind us of our favourite dish, a song that triggers memories from a different period in our lives, or seeing a person again and recounting experiences or emotions (good or bad). These are all retrieval cues, but they are unintentional and incidental retrieval cues.

Teachers have to plan and provide intentional retrieval cues to support the act of retrieving target memories in class. When we direct students to recall target memories this is intentional retrieval. The distinction between incidental and intentional is useful to be aware of, as there can be cues in a classroom environment that we don't realise prompt incidental retrieval.

We are constantly surrounded by potential retrieval cues, but we are not always reminded about our past; if that were the case daily life could become overwhelmed by past memories. When a student enters their classroom all of their memories from previous experiences and learning in that classroom don't come to mind. The reason for this is that people often have to be in a certain frame of mind to focus on the act of recall, which is known as 'retrieval mode'. When a retrieval task is carried out in class, students know they will be expected to recall prior learning and previously taught content therefore they adopt retrieval mode unknowingly.

Retrieval cues can come in many forms in the classroom, including verbal prompts from the teacher, sounds, icons, images and photos, and vocabulary. Cues are critical factors in determining what can be recalled from long-term memory. Evidence and experience tell us that younger learners need support, guidance and scaffolding in the initial stages of retrieval practice. Guidance, prompts, clues and hints are all techniques that can be used as retrieval cues.

McDermott and Roediger note that, 'The key to good retrieval is developing effective cues, ones that will lead the rememberer back to the encoded information.'[67] As we would gradually remove the structure and prompts for younger students as they progress, we do the same with retrieval cues. Ultimately, an effective retrieval cue will help students recall target memories with ease, confidence and accuracy. This isn't guaranteed due to various factors including the significance of retrieval strength (how accessible target memories are in long-term memory at a given point). Below are a range of tips, drawn from the evidence and my own classroom experience, to support designing effective retrieval cues.

The first piece of advice is to use the same or similar cues at the encoding and retrieval stages. The encoding stage, as discussed in chapter 1, is a vital part of the learning process and is directly linked to the retrieval stage. It is not possible to skip the encoding stage and it should not be rushed either. Anderson warns, 'If a memory is weakly encoded, even a good cue could be insufficient to trigger retrieval.'[68] Therefore, the more thoroughly we teach and explain content, as well as regularly checking for understanding, the more learners will reap those benefits later during the retrieval stage as they recall target memories.

The 'encoding specificity principle'[69] states that for a cue to be useful, it should be present at the encoding stage, although not all academics agree with Tulving on this. Despite the debate surrounding this principle, Anderson writes, 'Cues that are specifically encoded with a target are more powerful even if, on the face of it, they might seem less good than other cues that have a pre-existing relationship with the target.'[70] If students are given a retrieval cue that they have seen before this can increase their chances of retrieval success. Therefore, memory can be improved when information provided at the encoding stage is available at the retrieval stage as a cue to prompt the target memory.

---

67   McDermott, K. B. and Roediger, H. L. (2013). Memory (Encoding, Storage, Retrieval). In R. Biswas-Diener & E. Diener (Eds), Noba textbook series: *Psychology*. Champaign, IL: DEF publishers.

68   Baddeley, A., Anderson, M. C. and Eysenck, M. (2009). *Memory*. Hove, England: Psychology Press. Page 247.

69   Tulving, E., and Thomson, D. M. (1973). Encoding specificity and retrieval processes in episodic memory. *Psychological Review*, 80(5), 352–373.

70   Baddeley, A., Anderson, M. C. and Eysenck, M. (2009). *Memory*. Hove, England: Psychology Press. Page 246.

In chapter 3, I suggested using a knowledge organiser for retrieval purposes more so than encoding, and giving it to students and their families after the content has been taught. However, it is possible to use the cues from the KO in the encoding process; the terminology, information, and images can be used in lesson resources and then reintroduced later as retrieval cues.

Even if retrieval cues are not identical to those used at the encoding stage there should be relevance and a clear connection. It is important that retrieval cues are not obscure or abstract, and having retrieval cues does little good if they are unrelated to the target memory, as this can cause further confusion resulting in irrelevant information being recalled.[71] Anderson also wrote that, 'Retrieval can fail if cues are relevant, but are weak.'[72] Retrieval cues will vary in their strength and ability to support recall. This can depend on various factors, but the key is to ensure there is a link between retrieval cues being used and the information or the images provided at the encoding stage.

Anderson suggests that the use of elaboration in the encoding stage can have benefits because students can later associate the taught material to many cues at the retrieval stage. Retrieval does improve when more relevant cues are provided, for example, if something is on the 'tip of your tongue' perhaps all you need is a cue to recall that piece of information.

Although increasing retrieval cues can increase recall it is important teachers are aware of the 'cue overload principle'.[73] This suggests that a retrieval cue can lose its effectiveness in aiding recall of target memories when the amount of information provided by the retrieval cue increases. The more memories that are associated with a specific cue the less effective that cue will be when trying to recall a specific target memory.

If too many retrieval cues are provided, meaning too much support, then the challenge of retrieval practice is diluted and therefore not as effective. There is no set amount in terms of how much support should be provided with a retrieval cue, this is where the teacher must use their professional judgement and expertise. If a class or individual is

71   Baddeley, A., Anderson, M. C. and Eysenck, M. (2009). *Memory*. Hove, England: Psychology Press. Page 245.

72   Ibid. Page 246.

73   Watkins, O. C. and Watkins, M. J. (1975). Buildup of proactive inhibition as a cue-overload effect. *Journal of Experimental Psychology: Human Learning and Memory*, 1(4), 442-452.

struggling with retrieval practice then further cues, such as keywords written on the board or a verbal prompt from the teacher, can be provided. If the retrieval task is proving to be very easy for students to complete, it is likely there has been cue overload as there is a lack of challenge.

Acronyms and mnemonics can act as retrieval cues, supporting both working memory and long-term memory for students. Acronyms abbreviate words or phrases to letters so there is less to recall, while mnemonics provide a way to help students remember methods, concepts or other pieces of information. Both strategies can make information manageable for working memory by reducing how much there is to recall. They also provide cues to long-term memory to help students recall information. Most primary school teachers I have met are very creative with their use of mnemonics to help students with spellings of long or complex words.

The use of combining images and text at the encoding stage is known as multi-media learning or dual coding. This strategy provides two different representations of the information, making it more memorable and provides two ways of understanding the content (this is also an excellent strategy for EAL and SEND).

The use of dual coding at the encoding stage can be beneficial at the retrieval stage too. As dual coding supports encoding it can make that information stronger and more accessible. It also enables the teacher to remove either the text or images and use the other representation as a retrieval cue. As they will have seen this before when initially taught the material – but the accompanying part has been removed – students have to fill in that gap using their target memories.

Teachers can find the level of desirable difficulty and a form of differentiation by adding or removing cues. The diagram of the water cycle below is an example of how retrieval cues can be adapted for learners, to add support or increase challenge. A blank diagram can be provided for students to label or annotate. This would be challenging. To add further support the diagram could be labelled for students to write what they know about each stage of the process. Alternatively, the labels could be removed but with a list of the terms provided for students to select and place on the correct location on the diagram. The first letter of each label could be available as a prompt for students. There are many ways to add or remove retrieval cues.

It would be necessary for students to have seen this diagram at the encoding stage, which again links back to the encoding specificity principle. If a student is failing to recall target memories but others in the class are able to, an easy and effective way to differentiate and provide more support is simply to give the struggling student verbal prompts. I have done this many times by simply walking around the class and making observations.

I will offer a word of warning, based on my own experience of attempting to use the same cues at the encoding and retrieval stage that did not go to plan. When teaching about the World War One trenches, I showed students photographs which illustrated the living conditions and features of a trench. Images are often helpful visual aids. However, when using the same photo again in the retrieval stage and asking students to recall from memory information about the trenches, I found many were simply describing the photo. Answers included descriptions of the image, stating there were soldiers in uniform, sandbags and barbed wire. This was not the outcome I had planned for.

We can instruct students to go beyond description or we can increase the challenge, as shown below with an illustration of a trench (this can also be done with a photo) where students have to label or annotate with information, promoting recall over description.

A cue shouldn't provide the answer but instead ask questions or provide hints to lead the student in the right direction, while still promoting recall. This subtle form of differentiation is something teachers do day in and day out. We know our classes, we can identify when someone needs our help, and we develop the expertise to provide just the right amount of support needed to get students back on track.

Cued recall

I have included a range of examples of cued recall. The cues can be key words, sentence starters, images, icons or verbal prompts. If classroom displays contain information, then it is important to be aware that the displays can be acting as retrieval cues too.

Picture prompts

This task involves using images or icons as retrieval cues (the icons below are from the website www.nounproject.com). This provides students with guidance as to what the target memories they need to recall are. The icons or images must be clear – again it would be helpful if students have seen these before during the encoding stage – to ensure they are effective retrieval cues.

Example 1 is from a science lesson focusing on electricity. Further support could be provided with vocabulary for the circuit diagrams but again it is about striking a balance with retrieval cues providing support but avoiding the cue overload effect.

Symbol	What does the symbol represent? What can you remember?

Example 2 includes key images used on a Year 1 planets knowledge organiser and students have to recall what they can remember about each image from memory.

Image	How does each image link to our topic of planets? Explain from memory what you can remember.

Picture prompts can be used for both retrieval practice and providing opportunities for the application of knowledge, as shown below where students have to use their literacy knowledge correctly in a sentence with 'punctuation prompt'.

Punctuation	Use correctly in a sentence
.	I have a beautiful dog.
?	What is the name of your dog?
,	My dog is called Bruno, after the character from Encanto.
!	We don't talk about Bruno!

Fill in the blanks

This is a retrieval task that can be relatively easy as there is a lot of support and content already provided for students as they fill in the blanks. Therefore it is important that this type of task is still made challenging to ensure it is not a wasted retrieval opportunity. Fill in the blanks can be used with sentences, knowledge organisers, diagrams or a timeline as shown below.

Civil Rights Timeline: Fill in the blanks, some key dates have been provided to help you.

1955		1963	1965	1968
		"I have a dream.." speech delivered by MLK		Martin Luther King assassinated

Adding or removing cues will alter the level of challenge. How much support is provided depends on various factors, such as what point in the learning process the task is being completed; soon after encoding or towards the end of a topic? How in-depth is a student's knowledge of events and relevant information? Only essential or desirable knowledge should be included with the aim that students will eventually be able to create or verbally describe the timeline of key events from memory.

Word fragment completion is where part of a word is missing and students have to fill in the correct letters, focusing on vocabulary retrieval and an opportunity to practise spellings. This can be similar to a 'hangman' game approach.

Photo _____ thesis (Photosynthesis).

Word stem completion is when students have to complete the rest of the word, which can be useful for recalling tier three subject specific vocabulary. It is worth taking care with this as there are words that can have different letters to complete a word. For example, 'vol' could be volume, volcano, volcanic, volcanicity, voluntary, volt and more. However, when carried out in a specific context, such as a music or geography lesson, students are primed and more likely to recall the correct answer.

Free recall

As with any scaffolding approach, there will be a point where the scaffolding has gradually been reduced and eventually removed completely (or almost). In terms of retrieval practice, this is known as 'free recall'. Anderson writes, 'Free recall mimics situations in daily life in which we must produce a lot of information in no particular order.'[74] Free recall is challenging and demands more effort from students, but this adds to the effectiveness of the strategy. In a primary context I believe free recall tasks should be carried out towards the end of a topic or unit, once students have gained experience retrieving target memories and developed their subject knowledge, understanding and confidence.

A very simple and well known free recall retrieval task simply requires pen and paper. This is known as a 'brain dump' where students write down all they can from memory, no notes or checking with a partner are allowed. This is individual free recall. This can be challenging for students but does allow them an opportunity to elaborate and recall an extensive amount of knowledge from their long-term memory. This can be done across subjects and written brain dumps are suitable for key stages 1 and 2 whereas younger students in EYFS can carry out verbal brain dumps, speaking to their teacher or partner about what they can recall from memory. It is important to remember that with primary children this type of task should be completed towards the end of a topic or unit once students have had plentiful opportunities to retrieve information and will have developed their subject knowledge and confidence.

Brain dumps can combine information and images, asking students to write and sketch from memory relevant information linked to the topic. They can also be an extended answer, in the format of a mind map

---

74   Baddeley, A., Anderson, M. C. and Eysenck, M. (2009). *Memory*. Hove, England: Psychology Press. Page 258.

with different headings and categories or can be used to list key terms, key dates, key individuals and so on. A simple but flexible and versatile retrieval practice technique.

Retrieval grids

I created and shared retrieval grids several years ago, and they have been widely used and well received by teachers. Retrieval grids consist of questions based on prior learning. The initial grid I created and shared online had too many questions; this is before I was consciously aware of retrieval induced forgetting and the importance of only asking questions about essential or desirable knowledge. Although I am a history teacher I have seen numerous examples of this grid used in the primary classroom to promote daily maths recall.

Retrieval starter	
Last lesson:	Last week:
Last term:	Last year:

This grid can be used across all subjects but I think it does lend itself well to maths as a range of questions can be asked and it can be easier to be self-assessed and checked by the teacher, more so than extended answers would be. This is also ideal for a 'do now' starter task as there are only four questions (although more questions can be added). The example above doesn't have a reward mechanism, but you could award points; the further back the recalled content, the greater the number of points.

The only concern or piece of advice that I think is worth raising links back to retrieval strength. The question in the box 'Last year' should not ask a question that students haven't revisited in a whole year. There are some exceptions to this perhaps with multiplication where it is likely retrieval strength can be high if significant time and effort has been spent on it. If we ask students a question based on content not taught or discussed since a year ago this could prove to be very challenging as the retrieval strength would likely be low. Instead, questions asked in the 'Last term' box should eventually move to the 'Last year' box so although the content was taught a year ago it has been revisited since then.

Comic strips for sequencing and chronology

A comic strip is a classic classroom resource and it can be used in the encoding stage to consolidate knowledge and understanding of taught content, or it can be used at the retrieval stage, from memory. Comic strips work well when events are needed to be recalled in chronological order, such as in the study of history or the text of a story or play. This could also apply to a process, for example, asking students to recall a practical experiment or practical activity and the different stages involved.

Comic strips are an example of dual coding, combining images or illustrations with text. A comic strip can be a cued or free recall task, depending on whether any cues are provided or not.

Case study: Going beyond quizzing in the primary classroom with cued and free recall by Aidan Severs.

I connected with Aidan on social media and I continually learn a lot from him about effective and evidence-informed practices in the primary classroom. Aidan has shared his experience of using a variety of cued and free recall tasks to promote retrieval practice and illustrate how retrieval practice can and should be more than quizzing!

When it came to introducing retrieval practice into my primary school, concerns were raised about doing too much that resembled testing. Even though we understood the purpose and value of the testing effect, we wanted to keep teaching approaches varied, interesting and as low-stakes as possible. It was important for me as a leader to look beyond quizzing for alternative retrieval practice opportunities. I knew that no-quiz retrieval practice did not have to be a compromise - so long as the chosen activities were based on the core principles of retrieval practice.

Over the years that we developed our retrieval practice opportunities, teachers developed engaging and innovative ways of ensuring that children were learning key facts and vocabulary set out on our key fact sheets (our version of knowledge organisers). Although some of these approaches were based on quizzing most were based on the principles of either cued or free recall.

Many of the easiest to plan and deliver strategies are very simple. For example, cloze procedures were prepared quickly alongside the key facts: key words were removed from the facts, meaning that children had part of the wording of the fact to remind, or cue, them of the whole fact. Some of these were made into card games, or used as answer-to-progress questions in board games. As time went by some teachers adapted these cloze procedures to include fewer cues, meaning children had to remember more of the content themselves.

Card games were made to promote retrieval practice in vocabulary learning. Matching games were created, some with up to four matches where children have to match the word with its word class, definition and etymological root. Again, answer-to-progress question cards for use in board games were also created, meaning children have to define a word, or give a word for a definition, in order to move around the board.

Other simple approaches to cued recall are employed as lesson starters. Teachers use pictures and words to kick start whole class conversations focusing on retrieving information from previous content, including content from previous units of work, previous terms and previous years, especially where prior content is particularly relevant to the new content. Once the picture, word or phrase is introduced, teachers use further verbal prompts, including questioning, to continue the conversation, asking other children to elaborate, or to pick up on a new line of thinking that is introduced.

Although children like working together in the above ways, and often learn from each other while doing so, more individual approaches to cued and free recall can be taken too. For example, brain dump activities with a very basic prompt – 'write down (or tell me) all you can about the Romans in Britain' – give children the chance to think about what they know without other distractions, and allow them just to think (the whole purpose of retrieval practice). Older children take part in retrieve-taking activities where, instead of watching or listening to something and taking notes, they watch or listen and then write down what they remember – this has the dual advantage of allowing children to give their full attention to the content and then immediately having to begin to retrieve it. These retrieve-taking sessions often also involve peer collaboration where pairs of children add further information to each others' notes, or where children can walk the room collecting further information from their peers' notes in order to add to their own.

Some teachers also really enjoyed using mnemonics ('any learning technique that aids information retention or retrieval (remembering) in the human memory') as a type of retrieval practice – as did the children! One year group re-wrote Queen's *We Will Rock You* to include all their key facts in their Rocks and Soils unit. The song acted as a cue and children were able to recite all the key facts for the unit of work. Other teachers use student-created rhymes, acrostics and acronyms to help children to remember information. The fact that children make the connections and create the mnemonics themselves appears to help them to learn the content more easily, perhaps because they are having to think more about the information they are trying to remember.

The approaches outlined above, as well as others, were used to great effect. When speaking to children (the best form of assessment) it was clear that they were knowledgeable and able to recall the most important information for each unit of work they had undertaken. More than this, it appeared that because children had so easily been able to learn the information through retrieval practice activities, much time had been freed up to spend on using and applying that knowledge, and following their own lines of enquiry, often rooted in and prompted by the key facts that they had internalised.

Thank you to Aidan Severs for sharing so many great practical examples of retrieval practice in the primary classroom. You can follow Aidan on Twitter @AidanSevers and I recommend visiting his teaching and learning website www.aidansevers. com. Aidan is also available in his consultancy role to support primary schools and can be contacted via his website.

Free recall quizzing

Quizzing is often associated with multiple choice questions but quizzing can lend itself well to both cued and free recall. To increase the level of support when quizzing simply add cues, such as key words, images, audio or a verbal prompt from the teacher. To increase the level of challenge, remove the cues and support.

As previously mentioned I am reluctant to write an in-depth description of different online quizzing tools for retrieval practice, due to the pace of change with technology. Websites, apps and tools quickly develop and introduce new features. Technology evolves and improves at a rapid pace and that certainly applies to technology in education. Another reason I am reluctant to dedicate a chapter to this area (although it would certainly be possible and perhaps even a book in itself) is because access to technology across schools varies considerably. The introduction of online learning as a result of the pandemic has dramatically increased the use of technology with some educators embracing this and others keen to return to a classroom not dominated by technology. As with all approaches and techniques in education, there are pros and cons as well as benefits and limitations to using technology to enhance teaching and learning.

There is, however, one website that I will focus on and that is because at the time of writing, it is a very exciting time for Carousel Learning. Adam Boxer is a secondary science teacher and school leader, he is evidence-informed and like myself, is a big advocate for using retrieval practice inside and outside of the classroom. Adam created a resource called 'retrieval roulette' and after sharing and explaining how this worked via Twitter and his teaching blog, it quickly gained attention and interest from the teaching community. This was later developed to become the online quizzing platform Carousel (https://www.carousel-learning.com/) which has been growing in popularity since its creation. Adam wrote a case study about Carousel in my book *Retrieval Practice 2: Implementing, Embedding and Reflecting*. Since then Carousel has further developed and although Adam has a secondary background, Carousel has now expanded to support primary schools.

I attended a webinar hosted by members of the Carousel team where they explained how it can be used to support primary teachers and students with retrieval practice inside and outside of the classroom. I have also worked with primary teachers that speak very highly of Carousel and the many benefits they have noticed since joining its community.

Carousel has several features to support teachers with question design (free recall, cued recall and multiple choice questions), the quizzes can be used as low stakes revision or for low stakes testing. Passwords are not needed, students simply input their names and enter, this prevents login issues and if set as homework, not knowing a password is not a valid excuse!

The team at Carousel encourages teachers to create their own quizzes as this can be a useful process from a pedagogical and content knowledge perspective. Teachers can create and easily upload their own questions to Carousel. However – and this is what I think is brilliant – there is an option to use questions created by other teachers from the community banks in addition to using questions from quality assured question banks designed by the Carousel team to support the national curriculum.

There are currently thousands of questions available for primary teachers, covering different subjects across key stages 1 and 2, and no doubt over time this will continue to grow and develop even further. Every topic for science as part of the national curriculum is included in the Carousel question bank. Requests can also be made for further topics and questions, if unavailable in the question banks. There will be elements of the curriculum where questions banks are not included, such as 'My local history' but primary schools within the local community could easily collaborate on question and task design.

This is great in terms of workload, as teachers can create quizzes quickly and with ease without the quality being diminished. Another challenge at primary level is the breadth of subjects and topics taught, as when there is a focus on a knowledge rich curriculum, developing in-depth and rich subject knowledge in all areas can be difficult and time consuming. The question banks provide support and can be used by teachers early in their career, teachers lacking confidence or those who simply wish to further enhance and build on their existing subject knowledge. I would advise subject leads to review the question banks provided and share with colleagues as a form of support and professional development.

Carousel can be used in a lesson combined with mini white boards, known as 'whiteboard mode', which means it can be used in a lesson without students needing access to a device. The whiteboard mode allows the teacher to display questions to the class, and students write down their answers on mini white boards. If your school is limited in terms of technology, then this is ideal. The teacher can skim and scan a class set of answers and this can become part of a consistent classroom routine to practice recall. A 'do now' task which settles the class, involves low stakes retrieval practice and acts as a primer for the rest of the lesson. This feature is very user friendly for both the teacher and student. In terms of KS1, I would recommend the teacher reading the question and using mini white boards or 'hands up' to select the correct answer.

Online quizzes can also be set if students have access to devices in the classroom. There are no timers and I believe this is a good thing. As mentioned previously, students with SEND or EAL can need more time to process what the question is asking. For many students, question timers can equate to pressure and panic, and lead them to rush without reading the question carefully, making them likely to make more mistakes. Online quizzes set for classes can also shuffle questions, so question 1 for one student will be different to another student's question 1, to avoid conferring and cheating!

Carousel is also designed to support retrieval practice outside of the classroom and from my conversations with primary teachers and school leaders, for many this has been an area for development. Quizzes can be set and students can revise using the flashcards (questions are converted into flashcard format) and then when ready or confident they take the quiz. Carousel is very savvy and it does not allow the user (student) to have open the flashcard tab and the test in different browsers, this again prevents cheating or checking.

Students can take a quiz more than once. Adam insists on his class achieving a minimum of 80% and they should keep going until they do so. I agree this is a good target as it shows a high success rate, which is vital with retrieval practice. If students are scoring much lower than 80% there are several factors that could be the reason, but it is likely to be that the questions are too challenging, or the student may not be concentrating or trying. If all students score very highly, especially on the first attempt, then it is likely the questions were too easy and lacked challenge. The sweet spot involves desirable difficulty; we want students to think hard and push themselves to recall information, but we also want them to experience successful recall.

Another feature of Carousel that I thought was simple but brilliant, was the ability to combine questions from different year groups on specific topics. For example, a class has studied plants in Year 4 and then again in Year 6, the questions asked in Year 4 can be embedded and combined with questions relevant to Year 6 content. This is drawing on long-term learning and memory as well as making links and connections across the curriculum, thus boosting retrieval strength for previously covered topics. This is also useful for a teacher that is a Year 6 specialist as they can easily access and include questions from another year group, even if they did not teach that content to that year group.

Carousel is once again workload friendly in terms of marking and feedback. Students will be shown the answer from the quiz and then compare it with their response to select if it was correct or incorrect. If students are incorrect the correct answer is shown to them. If students think they can select they were right, when they weren't, then they will get caught out as the teacher can oversee how students self-assess their answers. If a teacher notices a misconception or an answer that they want to address with the class in the lesson, they can select the star button and it becomes visibly highlighted for the teacher as interesting and will be flagged up for later reference. There is a soft deadline, especially useful if setting Carousel for homework but this is for reference for the teacher and to inform the student when the quiz should be completed by.

If you want to find out more you can scan the code at the back of this book or visit https://www.Carousel-learning.com. You can follow Adam Boxer on Twitter @adamboxer1.

Going beyond factual recall

Many teachers I have worked with have told me they find themselves mainly using retrieval practice for factual recall. Factual recall is important and well suited to retrieval tasks and quizzes. However, if we remember the learning process and that retrieval practice isn't the final stage, students need to be able to apply and transfer the knowledge they can recall. To help with this I created a retrieval practice pyramid; as the level of challenge increases with each layer of the pyramid, the points also increase.

The bottom layer of the pyramid is important and shouldn't be skipped, instead the questions asked should provide support for the questions higher up. For example, if studying the story *Charlotte's Web* before asking a question about how it is shown that Fern feels responsible for Wilbur, the students have to show that they understand and can recall the correct meaning of responsibility. Hence, the questions create building blocks to reach the questions above.

Retrieval Practice Pyramid

The Circulatory System

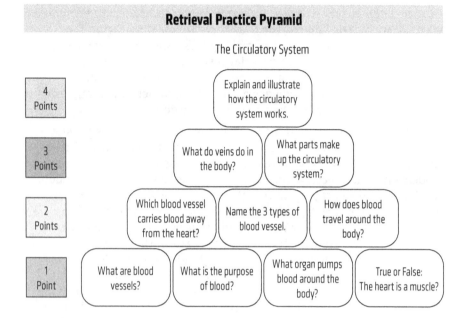

Retrieval relay

I created this task because although my students enjoy collaborating, the act of retrieval must always be individual. This task ensures individual recall and collaboration among peers. Students write in the first box what they can from memory about a specific topic, another student will complete the second box adding further content. Everyone in the class is always filling in a box, they swap and share their sheet like a relay baton.

Retrieval Relay Race!

Instructions: In the first box **write as much as you can remember** about our topic. In the second box one of your peers must write what they can recall about our topic **but they cannot repeat any of the information from your first box**! The third box needs to be completed by someone else but again this must include new information and the same for the final box.

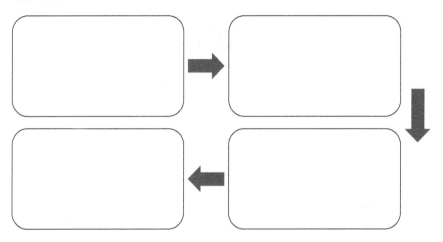

This task can take longer than some of the others as students are expected to read all the other responses, so as to not repeat anything, and by the time students need to complete the fourth box it can be very tough!

Individual spotlight

In the first chapter I shared 'keyword spotlight' where the retrieval questions all focused on one key term. This idea is the same concept, but all the questions focus on one key individual. The idea is that all questions home in on the individual studied, and they become the target memory. The questions can be adapted based on the essential and desirable knowledge required.

Individual Spotlight

What can you remember about this individual?	Florence Nightingale 	How is this individual linked to our topic? Explain.

What adjectives would you use to describe this individual?	Self assess: How confident you are recalling information about this individual?

Think and link

This task allows the opportunity for factual recall of knowledge but then encourages students to make, establish and explain connections. The connections can be with key events or individuals as shown below.

Retrieval Practice: Think & Link

What can you recall about MLK?	What can you recall about Rosa Parks?

Explain how MLK and Rosa Parks are connected.

This can be used across a range of subjects where connections exist and are worth exploring, or that students should be able to identify, understand and recall.

Thinking and linking grids

The 6x6 grid is credited to Steve Bowkett and I first discovered this activity in the book *Outstanding Teaching: Engaging Learners* by Andy Griffith and Mark Burns. I have adapted this 6x6 grid in many ways to support retrieval practice. This resource is not always low effort for the teacher as 36 boxes need to be filled with relevant content! However, it can work very well in the classroom.

Students work in pairs and dice are required. A student will roll the dice (either two dice or roll one dice twice) and if the first set of numbers are three and four the student will explain how poverty links to *A Christmas Carol*. Students roll again and then try to make a link between the first factor, in this case poverty, and the second factor selected randomly by the dice. Students can verbally explain the link or write and record the link in a format like the example below that was created and shared by English teacher and author Stuart Pyrke @SPryke2 on Twitter.

'A Christmas Carol' Thinking and Linking Grid

	1	2	3	4	5	6
1	Scrooge	Light	Tiny Tim	Marley's chains	Memory	Forgiveness
2	Family	The Ghost of Christmas Yet to Come	Scrooge as a school boy	Martha Cratchit	Fan	Peter Cratchit
3	Gratitude	Christmas	Reform	Poverty	Cold	The Ghost of Christmas Past
4	Marley's ghost	The charity collectors	Bob Cratchit	Ignorance and Want	Mrs Cratchit	Generosity
5	Hope	The Ghost of Christmas Present	Compassion	The workhouse	Redemption	Fezziwig
6	Repentance	Isolation	Belle	Responsibility	Fred	Guilt

Links Made

Box 1	Box 2	Link between the two

This can be very difficult and is best carried out once students have a solid and secure knowledge base so they are able to establish and explain links. Some factors on the grid link more easily than others therefore the challenge can vary significantly. There will be some obvious links but students have surprised me with carefully crafted connections they have made and explained.

Retrieval cues play a key role in the process of retrieval practice. Understandably, younger students often need more retrieval cues but the fact that retrieval cues can come in many forms in the classroom is something the teacher should use to their advantage. Free recall is harder for primary students but it's important not to shy away from that challenge and instead recognise when the time is right to use free recall, whether that is verbally or through written responses.

Further recommended reading

The Ingredients for Great Teaching. Pedro De Bruyckere. (2018)

Rosenshine's Principles in Action. Tom Sherrington. (2019)

Teaching WalkThrus 2: Five-step guides to instructional coaching. Oliver Caviglioli and Tom Sherrington. (2021)

100 Ideas for Primary Teachers: Maths. Shannen Doherty. (2021)

CHAPTER 6
VERBAL RETRIEVAL PRACTICE

Speaking and listening are at the heart of every classroom, whether it is the teacher speaking or listening or the students speaking or listening. This happens day in, day out in every classroom. There are some students who can express their answers verbally better than they can do through writing and feel more confident responding this way. This is not true of all students, but those who prefer to verbally recall over writing we must support to build confidence and skills with written literacy while allowing them to continue to use verbal recall.

Verbal retrieval practice strategies have many noticeable benefits for younger learners, as well as students with SEND or EAL members of the class. I've been fortunate to have had many conversations with EYFS practitioners and KS1 teachers, as well as observing lessons with younger students. Retrieval practice plays an essential role from an early age as Agarawal and Fazio noted, 'Recent work suggests that younger children also benefit from retrieval-based learning. In fact, even infants benefit from retrieval!'[75]

At EYFS learners are often unable to read complex questions or write elaborative answers therefore teachers find alternative ways to promote recall in the classroom. This is mainly achieved through verbal opportunities, activities and learning games and play. Verbal retrieval practice should continue throughout a child's education as it is an important part of the recall process and allows opportunities to rehearse, practice and develop pronunciation and oracy skills as well as reaping the benefits of the act of retrieving information from long-term memory.

The *Statutory framework for the early years foundation stage: Setting the standards for learning, development and care for children from birth to five* published by the DfE in 2021 makes clear the importance of verbal communication with young learners. The framework states that, 'Children's back-and-forth interactions from an early age form the

---

75   Fazio, L. K. and Agarwal, P. K. (2020). How to implement retrieval-based learning in early childhood education. *Retrievalpractice.org* Available at: http://pdf.retrievalpractice.org/EarlyChildhoodGuide.pdf

foundations for language and cognitive development. The number and quality of the conversations they have with adults and peers throughout the day in a language-rich environment is crucial.'[76] These conversations will involve students asking questions, sharing their thoughts, feelings, opinions and ideas as well as answering questions and recalling information from long-term memory.

Communication is also at the heart of students developing their vocabulary, something which is discussed more thoroughly in the next chapter. The framework adds that children at the expected level of development should be able to demonstrate understanding of what has been read to them by retelling stories and narratives using their own words and recently introduced vocabulary. Again, this is a key aspect of retrieval practice.

EYFS is truly a unique key stage in terms of learning, progress and social, emotional and physical development. An exciting and crucial time in the development and progress of children. Nursery school headteacher Julian Grenier explains the influence and paramount importance of EYFS. Grenier writes in *Working with the revised Early Years Foundation Stage. Principles into Practice:*

> *The practitioners who work in the early years guide and shape young children. They create a sense of friendly co-operation. They also set clear rules and limits. This shows that they value each child as an individual, and help each child to live and learn alongside others. They play and have conversations with children. This is how practitioners help children to manage and enjoy being a group, share and take turns. In the early years, children learn new vocabulary and knowledge across different areas of learning. They learn to decide what they want to do, and how to solve different problems along the way. These experiences help them to develop skills which will benefit them throughout their education, and the rest of their lives.*[77]

Conversations and verbal retrieval practice are at the essence of EYFS teaching and learning.

---

76 Department for Education (2021). *Statutory framework for the early years foundation stage.* DfE. Available at: https://assets.publishing.service.gov.uk/government/uploads/system/uploads/attachment_data/file/974907/EYFS_framework_-_March_2021.pdf

77 Grenier, J. (2020). *Working with the revised Early Years Foundation Stage.* Principles into Practice. Sheringham Nursery School and Children's Centre. Available at: http://development-matters.org.uk/wp-content/uploads/2020/10/Working-with-the-revised-Early-Years-Foundation-Stage-Principles-into-Practice-.pdf

Case study: Verbal retrieval practice in reception at Jerry Clay Academy.

Retrieval in the early years; use of the learning journey by Jerry Clay Academy. I have had the privilege to learn from and collaborate with staff at Jerry Clay Academy and they have very kindly agreed to share one of the strategies they use to promote verbal retrieval practice with younger children.

Children in the early years have the benefit of an environment which blends practical, real-life opportunities across seven areas of learning. As an academy, we are passionate about providing our children with retrieval opportunities, both reactively and planned to ensure that key learning becomes committed to short, then long-term memory. An area which we felt needed more thought and precision using retrieval practices was in the early years. We really needed to think more deeply about how we allow our children to remember their learning and make connections over time. Over the last couple of years, our children have used a learning board in the EYFS to capture their most pertinent learning stories over half a term.

Over time it became obvious that more precision was needed to ensure key learning points were captured. We recognised that we had been taking a very dispersed approach to gathering information, with little thought to next steps. It was important that we enabled our children to commit learning to memory and then sustain learning at a much deeper level so that it became more memorable over time. We saw the importance of reducing the learning down to one week with prior learning references.

Elements which were key to the success of retrieval in early years

1. 'In the moment' additions to the learning journey board throughout the week

Staff add photographs and annotations to the board over the course of one week. Our decision to only include one week was due to our belief that the board could become cognitively overloaded for the children and become meaningless, almost wallpaper. Our aim is to ensure that everything on the board has meaning and allows our children to make connections to prior learning. Children transcribe the importance of their learning, be this in a child- or adult-initiated activity and these are attached as visual prompts to the board. By allowing our children to explain their learning, it begins to make sense to them and embeds in their short-term memory. Having a visual representation on the board every day allows for them to make these connections.

2. Teachers making reference to the learning board every day during planning time

When children are planning the learning they intend to do in areas of provision, both inside and outside, the teacher scaffolds the prior learning that has taken place. In order to develop sustained learning, the teacher will draw reference to children's comments and how they could make a connection to the next step on their learning journey.

3. Collectively coming together in 'gathering time' to review the learning at the end of the week

Children come together as a whole group to review the key learning points, for example the planting of herbs in the mud kitchen, and the teacher uses a number of strategies to embed the learning.

An example of one such strategy is providing scaffolding. Throughout the session the teacher provides scaffolding to help the children remember. We find that precise questioning during planning and review sessions is essential not only for our children to make sense of their learning but also for them to think about next steps. We have found that when children do not benefit from retrieval-based learning, it is often because they were unable to retrieve any of the relevant information. By scaffolding their recall, the teacher helps children to recall more information. For example, instead of asking broad questions like, 'What do you remember about planting our herbs today?' teachers provide additional prompts, such as 'What do you remember about the steps we took to plant our herbs today?'

We found that broad open-ended questions like 'What have we learned about planting herbs?' can be difficult for younger children and made retrieval practice too difficult. We recognised that getting the balance of questioning right for children was key. If we make the questions too easy, the depth of retrieval becomes too superficial too.

Allowing children to use previous learning to make connections for future learning

Using cognitive-processing language to help with retrieval

We have learned through this approach that over time, 'teacher talk' which includes retrieval practice, strategy suggestions and questions that make children think about their own learning, is hugely beneficial. Described as 'cognitive-processing language' by researchers, exposure to this type of teacher talk has improved our children's memory abilities and their learning. Examples of cognitive-processing language include deliberate memory demands (Who can remember the first step we took to build a bridge for the goats?), strategy suggestions (If you are having trouble thinking of ways to build the bridge, you can look at the diagram to help you.), and requests for children to think about their thinking (How did you figure out which pieces you would need to build a sturdy bridge for the goats so that the troll doesn't get them?). This cognitive-processing language has been particularly important for the children's ability to strategically solve problems.

Speaking frames to support retrieval

We use a number of speaking frames for our children to use when relaying their learning. This model has allowed our children, over time, to get into the habit of evaluating their learning, making connections and commiting the learning to memory.

The most important benefit of our approach to retrieval in the early years is that children recognise that their play is valued, they are encouraged to make sense of what they are doing and that this provides powerful learning to inform their next steps.

Thank you to the staff at Jerry Clay Academy for sharing their experiences and expertise.

The production effect

Authors of the article *The production effect in memory: multiple species of distinctiveness*, Michal Icht, Yaniv Mama and Daniel Algom explain that 'the production effect' refers to the difference in memory, favouring words read aloud in contrast to words read silently during study.[78] Studies have shown that reading words aloud during the encoding stage can support memory during retrieval.

The abstract from a key study published in 2013 states, 'The production effect is the finding that subsequent memory is better for words that are produced than for words that are not produced.'[79] To produce, means to do something with the information read, therefore reading the information out loud in contrast to silence. This requires more effort as the learner is reading, saying, pronouncing and hearing the text. Many other studies have suggested the production effect can support long-term memory, for both encoding and retrieval as it can lead to improved recall of word lists and paragraphs of text studied.[80] There will be times where silent reading is more appropriate but if reading text or information that needs to be recallable at a later date, reading out loud can support the recall.

Retrieval practice tennis

No tennis balls or racquets are required! This is a verbal retrieval practice game students carry out in pairs or small groups and can be used for students across different key stages. The concept is that students take it in turns to recall something connected to the topic when instructed by the teacher. For example, in maths this could be numbers, factors or multiplication with student one saying 'five', student two saying 'ten' then back to student one with '15' and so on. This can be done with letters or categories linked to a topic studied. If a class were studying rocks, the pairs can take it in turns to recall vocabulary linked to this, or different types of rocks.

The game was played regularly in my class when I taught second language Welsh. This was great as it allowed the verbal recall of different key terms such as foods, colours, and animals all in Welsh,

---

78   Icht, M., Mama, Y. and Algom, D. (2014). The production effect in memory: multiple species of distinctiveness. *Front. Psychol.* 5:886.

79   Quinlan, C. K. and Taylor, T. L. (2013). Enhancing the production effect in memory. *Memory*, 21:8, 904-915.

80   Ozubko, J. D., Hourihan, K. L. and MacLeod, C. M. (2012). Production benefits learning: The production effect endures and improves memory for text. *Memory*, 20:7, 717-727.

which also helped develop oracy and pronunciation. Students cannot repeat themselves or say something their partner has already said. Scores can be kept but it should be low stakes, and even better is no stakes where the students aren't in competition with others but instead are trying to keep the retrieval volley going for as long as they can together.

This is a quick recall task that is low effort for the teacher but promotes high impact verbal retrieval practice. An image or keyword can be displayed on the board or a verbal instruction can be given by the teacher, 'This round of retrieval tennis you will have to recall different examples of animals'. I enjoyed walking around the class listening to students and then later discussing as a class what was recalled during the verbal volley, and being able to provide verbal feedback immediately.

Walkabout bingo

This verbal retrieval task can be too difficult for younger learners if they struggle to read and ask the questions on the sheet. The purpose of 'Walkabout bingo' is for students to verbally answer questions based on previously taught content, but it also encourages students to talk to one another, going beyond the typical think, pair and share as they have to engage with different members of the class.

It is simple to create and very adaptable for different subjects, and the number of questions can easily be altered. The questions included should only require short answers. Students can only ask their peers one question, then record their answer and name and move on. The first person to have all their questions answered shouts 'Bingo!' and the teacher can go through the answers for students to mark with a tick or cross.

To ensure students don't just ask the same people in the class they have to record the name of the student that provided them with the answer on the sheet in the same box as the answer. If a student thinks the answer they have been given by a peer is incorrect they don't have to write it down and can ask someone else. Below is an example of walkabout bingo in a music lesson.

Q1. Name an instrument that belongs to the string family. Answer: Name:	Q2. Give an example of an instrument that does not have strings. Answer: Name:	Q3. What family is the flute a member of? Answer: Name:
Q4. What does rhythm mean? Answer: Name:	Q5. What is a chord? Answer: Name:	Q6. What does pitch describe? Answer: Name:
Q7. Give an example of a percussion instrument. Answer: Name:	Q8. What is the name of words that make up a song? Answer: Name:	Q9. What does tempo mean? Answer: Name:
Q10. What is a beat? Answer: Name:	Q11. What is a group of singers called? Answer: Name:	Q12. What is the melody? Answer: Name:

Verbal questioning techniques in the classroom

Questioning is present in every classroom, in every lesson, every day. There is both an art and science to planning and asking questions in class, and just as with so much else in teaching, these must be learned. Asking questions can happen at every stage in the learning process from checking for understanding and eliciting evidence of learning to retrieval practice and elaboration with application and transfer.

There are benefits of using both closed and open questions in the classroom and all can be used for verbal recall, but higher order questions require more thinking time for students. Teachers should share, discuss and develop questions alongside colleagues.

Examples of closed questions:

A. What is the name of the holy book in Christianity?

B. What are followers of Christianity known as?

C. What is the symbol of Christianity?

These short answer questions can be asked verbally with 'cold calling' (discussed below) or written responses on mini white boards. Question C could be answered with students drawing the symbol of a cross. These are often the easiest type of questions for teachers to create and ask.

An open question requires some explanation and elaboration from students, often short answers won't suffice.

Example of open questions:

D. Why do Christians celebrate Christmas?

E. How do Christians celebrate Christmas?

F. What Christmas traditions are not Christian traditions?

Higher order questions again require retrieval and elaboration, but they go beyond short answer responses and require a more complex and detailed answer. They can be difficult to answer well but they do enable students to be stretched and challenged. Higher order questions should be asked when students have developed secure subject knowledge and understanding.

Example of higher order questions:

G) Describe how Christians practise their religion and faith.

H) How does the Bible help Christians practise their religion and faith?

I) Describe the teachings and messages shared by Jesus Christ.

Dylan Wiliam has written extensively about the use of questioning in the classroom. In the book *Embedded Formative Assessment*[81] he offers this simple advice to teachers when asking higher order questions:

Plan it.   Ask it.   Be quiet.

This advice can apply to all questions but there will be times in the lesson when teachers ask unplanned responsive questions to students.

Cold calling questioning

A common occurrence in the classroom is when a teacher asks a question and hands go up; often some, not all hands. It is not possible during a question and answer session in class to hear from every individual, it would take too long and be difficult to do. Most classes have the eager or confident students that are always keen to volunteer answers or opinions and other students who are content for their peers to answer as they stay quiet. Teachers can encourage other members of the class to get involved but it can be a struggle.

There is a time and place for a questioning approach with hands up, but it is not effective for verbal retrieval practice as all learners need to be engaged in the retrieval process. The obvious benefit of a mini white board is that the teacher can ask a question and instead of hearing the answer from one student they can see in front of them the answers from every member of the class. This doesn't mean that opportunities can't be created for verbal retrieval practice in the classroom.

Cold calling is a no hands up questioning strategy where the teacher asks a question and instead of students volunteering to answer the question the teacher selects who will answer. Many teachers already use this no hands up questioning approach but perhaps are not familiar with the term 'cold calling'. Students should understand that with cold

81   Wiliam, D. (2011). *Embedded Formative Assessment*. Bloomington, IN: Solution Tree Press.

calling they could potentially be asked a question during the lesson. This keeps the learners engaged and prepared and ensures they are paying attention and actively involved.

A misunderstanding of cold calling is that it is picking on children and forcing them to answer questions verbally in class. This is not true as it aims to be an inclusive classroom approach which tells the class that their teacher doesn't want to just hear from a select few students, and that the voice of every learner in the classroom is valued and should be heard. The teacher has the power to decide which questions to ask and who should answer them. For example if there is a student who is reluctant to answer a knowledge-based question in front of their peers for fear of getting it wrong, the teacher could ask for their opinion or thoughts on the matter, meaning there is no wrong answer. Or the teacher could ask an easier question to provide an opportunity for successful recall and to boost confidence and motivation, and then gradually increase the level of challenge and difficulty.

Tips for using cold calling in the primary classroom

Ask a student more than once – Make sure to ask students a question more than once so they don't assume that once they've been asked a question they can switch off, as they need to stay focused throughout the lesson. This can help with concentration, effort and attention as students will all be thinking about the answer even if they are not the chosen student.

Ensure cold calling is positive – It should never appear that teachers are trying to catch students out with a 'gotcha' moment. Although students are being held to account with this technique it should never be used to humiliate or embarrass, that doesn't have a place in any classroom. Cold calling is a great opportunity to provide genuine praise and encouragement to students.

Wait time must be provided – The teacher should ask the question then pause, allowing some wait and thinking time for the students. After the wait time the teacher can select the student to answer. The amount of wait time provided will vary with different classes and even different topics and styles of question.

I observed Lowri Williams, teacher of Year 1 and 2 at Ysgol Rhoscolyn, cold calling students focusing on multiplication. As students had been spending a lot of time on multiplication and their retrieval strength was high, they were able to respond quickly and didn't require a long wait time. In contrast, in geography when Lowri was asking questions to find out what students could recall about Brazil, the wait time was increased as the retrieval strength was not as high as with multiplication due to various factors, the main one being that maths is rehearsed daily in contrast to geography. Lowri has mastered cold calling with her class using her expertise, professional judgement and in-depth knowledge of her students. Teachers often don't realise how brilliant they are and how they use effective classroom routines with ease based on their knowledge and skills.

Make cold calling the norm in your classroom and school – Make cold calling a regular daily classroom routine. It's even better if it becomes the norm across the whole school as part of the teaching and learning culture.

Observe others cold calling – It can be a good idea to watch other teachers carry out cold calling. It could be your colleagues or there are plenty of examples online. This helped me significantly as I initially struggled with the approach after years of relying on hands up! Another useful strategy is to seek feedback about your use of cold calling in the classroom. Ask a colleague to give you feedback about your questioning; perhaps you aren't providing enough thinking time or are targeting the same students without realising it because you suspect they will have the correct answer.

Cold calling can be combined with think-pair-share – The teacher will ask a question and allow adequate think time for individual retrieval and recording. This could be students writing down their thoughts or answers in their books or on a mini white board. The individual thinking time is essential to ensure every student is going through the process of retrieval practice.

After the individual think time the students can discuss their answer with their partner with 'compare in a pair'. After they have had time to discuss their answer and ideas the teacher can cold call and select students to share their answer with the rest of the class. This is a good technique because at the point of cold calling students have had time to think about their answer and discuss it with someone else, meaning they are likely to be more confident to share with others.

Although cold calling isn't an opportunity to hear from every learner in the class, it can be useful for verbal retrieval practice as long as it is used alongside other opportunities to practise recall.

What's your best answer?

I have been very fortunate to spend time at Ysgol Rhoscolyn in Anglesey, North Wales. I have observed lessons, returning later to observe the same teachers and classes, as well as have conversations with the children and deliver training to the teachers. Rwth Davies is an experienced teacher at Ysgol Rhoscolyn and I have thoroughly enjoyed sitting in on her lessons (I quickly realised why her students think very highly of her and love her lessons). Rwth encourages a lot of verbal discussion in her classroom. This classroom context is unusual as lessons are bilingual, some are taught in Welsh and others in English, so verbal practice is necessary to develop confidence and oracy in both languages.

During an art lesson with Rwth there was a series of questions for students to answer. The questions were a combination of recall, understanding and an opportunity to express emotions and demonstrate creativity. There were questions about how the artwork made the students feel. There were questions about what they noticed and what stood out to them. There were also questions about the artist and making links and connections with prior learning. In a creative subject such as art there is certainly a place for retrieval practice, but it can be embedded and combined with the creative elements of the subject, not isolated as a bolted on task, as Rwth was able to effectively demonstrate.

The questions were on a sheet and students had time to think, discuss with their peers and write down their individual responses and answers. After completing the written questions, Rwth wanted students to share their responses during a class discussion. Some members of the class were desperate to share their answers verbally, whereas others were shy and reluctant to do so (an experience many teachers can relate to).

To encourage everyone to share their answers verbally Rwth cold called students instead of using a hands up approach and asked them to share their best answer. This was clearly a strategy Rwth had used before and one with which the students were familiar. It proved excellent at promoting verbal responses because students had been given time to think, time to discuss and compare their thoughts with a partner, time to write down their answers and finally were being asked to share their best answer; all those techniques combined helped to build up confidence in reluctant, shy or nervous students. They didn't feel on the spot as Rwth had given them control as to what they would share with the rest of the class; the answer they felt the most comfortable and confident with. Their best answer.

Rwth then asked further questions, prompting lots of elaboration and combining retrieval practice with observation and interpretations of the artwork. This is why it is so fascinating to observe other teachers. To her this was a simple method of questioning her students to encourage participation and discussion, to her perhaps nothing special or extraordinary. I, as the observer, was in awe of how she was able to draw out such wonderful and detailed verbal answers from students who, if only offered a hands up approach, would clearly never volunteer to answer a question or share an opinion.

If students are struggling with confidence or reluctant to engage in verbal discussions and questioning in the classroom then asking them for their best answer is a great way to involve them; reducing what may feel like high stakes or pressure and providing an opportunity for further elaboration and genuine praise. Diolch Rwth.[82]

Please indulge me as I share a brief anecdote about my experience of being a second language Welsh speaker. I have lived in Wales for most of my life and as other people from Wales can attest to; not all Welsh people can speak Welsh. Sadly, my family and close friends do not speak Welsh. I attended an English medium school, but it was compulsory (and still is) for students in Wales to learn Welsh.

I embraced this at school, performing well at GCSE and choosing to study Welsh second language at A Level, which involved the study of Welsh literature and involved developing skills in speaking, listening, reading and writing. I then attended Aberystwyth University in Wales and I lived in Welsh speaking accommodation with other students during my first year of study. I consider myself a confident and able Welsh speaker, but not fluent.

During an interview for a teaching position at the start of my career, the questions were asked through a combination of English and Welsh (that is very unusual and has only happened to me on that one occasion). I found the whole experience very distressing. The questions asked to me in English, I could respond to in English, and I felt I coped well with this although I was still very nervous as a job interview is high stakes and intense.

---

82   *Diolch is Welsh for thank you.

When the questions were asked in Welsh, this was awful. I did manage to understand them, but my responses took longer to formulate and give. I was searching in my memory for words, terms and phrases I wanted to use; some I could eventually recall, whereas others I did not know, so my answers weren't as sophisticated as they could have been. This added another layer of pressure to an already stressful situation. Not being able to answer in my first language meant the process was slower, more challenging, frustrating and did not reflect my true abilities.

I did not get the job. It was no surprise when I was told I was unsuccessful, and I sobbed. On reflection, I think the tears were more as a result of going through the gruelling interview experience rather than being unsuccessful. As I said, this is just an story about a part of my life but it has provided me with an empathy about trying to communicate in a language that is not your first, or one you are not fluent in.

I was not as quick at answering questions because in my mind I was translating words, searching for vocabulary in my second language repertoire and becoming annoyed at not being able to say in Welsh what I could say in English. I imagine students with English as an additional language may experience some of these same challenges too but on a more frequent basis than I have.

This is another reason why stressing the low stakes nature of retrieval practice is vital. If any student believed they were being tested daily that could result in stress and a dislike of school, but imagine doing so daily in a language that is not your first. School life and learning will bring challenges for EAL students, but retrieval practice can and should help them. I would stress the removal of question timers with quizzes as some EAL students may need longer to process and understand what the question is asking, and may take longer to find the vocabulary and language that is required.

It is very important to provide plentiful opportunities for verbal retrieval practice for EAL students. In my school in Abu Dhabi, the curriculum and lessons are delivered through English but the cohort of students are very diverse, coming from all over the world, including many for whom English is not their first or even second language. I can recall teaching a Year 7 class and two boys would often write very basic responses during retrieval tasks, Arabic was their first language and English their second. I noticed their struggles and monitored this, regularly offering support and checking for their understanding in lessons.

Up until that point all the main retrieval practice tasks I had set at the start of lessons had been quizzes or written tasks. This time I set a verbal retrieval task and I purposefully stood near the two boys that had been struggling. I was blown away by their responses; they were able to verbally recall a lot of accurate and detailed information and they both did so with ease and confidence. Their retrieval strength was high. I listened then asked them further questions which they were able to answer and elaborate on. This was a great opportunity for me to hear how they could successfully recall information. I was able to praise their efforts and achievements. This was a boost to their confidence and motivation in contrast to previous tasks where their written responses had been brief and limited. This was a significant turning point for me, although I was aware that written communication was an area for their development, this experience highlighted that written literacy was the main concern and that the students had been understanding content and were able to recall it too.

For further information, resources and support for EAL learners I recommend visiting The Bell Foundation website: https://www.bell-foundation.org.uk/. The Bell Foundation declares that their aims are to improve policy, practice and systems to enable children, adults and communities in the UK that speak English as an additional language to overcome disadvantage through language education.

In primary the formal assessments of SATs, or national reading and numeracy tests in Wales, are in written form, as are most examinations at secondary. This could be a reason to explain why there can often be more emphasis on written work and recall over verbal. However, in learning and in life, if we want to verbally articulate thoughts, opinions and answers, recall is a crucial skill. It is important that teachers provide students with opportunities for both written and verbal recall. Observers (whether that be line managers, leaders, governors, parents or inspectors) can view a child's book and make inferences about their learning but it would be much more effective to talk to the child about their learning and listen to them. There is value at looking at evidence of written work and often progress is visible from one page to another but that alone isn't enough. The voice of the learner should be heard, something which is true for retrieval practice and verbal recall.

I sat with a group of children in Year 4 at Ysgol Rhoscolyn on Anglesey in North Wales and we looked at their art and design sketchbooks together. We discussed artwork and topics, I was able to ask questions about their prior learning and they were able to confidently answer and explain. This was a very interesting and informative conversation, and I was able to listen to the students verbally recall information about their prior learning in detail and with enthusiasm. Talking to students about prior learning is a great retrieval opportunity and is something students can do with their peers and family members at home.

Early childhood specialist and author Marianne Sargent writes in her book *100 Ideas for Early Years Practitioners. Observation, Assessment & Planning* about the power of photo observations with EYFS. Sargent writes, 'Photos make great snapshot observations, particularly when recording a child's transient creative achievements. For example, a child may build an intricate model using wooden blocks. A quick snap of the model before it is cleared away, and the practitioner has a permanent record.'[83] These photo snapshots of learning can be used as a retrieval cue to prompt learners to verbally recall prior learning. It is important to focus on the learning rather than the task that produced it; we don't want students to be able to recall doing a worksheet but be unable to tell us anything about what they learned from it. Photos trigger memories in our personal lives, and we can harness this in the classroom for verbal retrieval practice.

Another conversation that stands out was with Amelia in Year 6 at Myddelton College, Denbigh. Amelia talked me through her prior learning in science and English, using her exercise book as a prompt. When she showed me her science assessment I asked if she knew how that assessment was different to retrieval practice. To my surprise and delight Amelia was able to explain the difference between regular retrieval practice she does in class to the assessment they complete less regularly. She also told me that in her previous school they sometimes did quizzing but not every day, as they do at Myddelton College. Amelia said at first this seemed unusual but she knows she has made a lot of progress as a result. It was incredible to listen to a student talk so eloquently and passionately about their own learning.

Dyfan in Year 1 at Myddelton College was very keen to tell me he understood the differences between short-term and long-term memory. This clearly wasn't a rehearsed or scripted answer because I quizzed him on long-term memory! I was blown away by his response and understanding of learning. Dyfan said he wanted to read my retrieval practice books but I told him he doesn't need to! Students that

---

83   Sargent, M. (2018). *100 Ideas for Early Years Practitioners: Observation, Assessment & Plan-ning*. London: Bloomsbury. Page 25.

understand how learning happens have a huge advantage and control over their own learning and progress.

The final chapter of this book focuses on sharing the benefits of retrieval practice and different strategies with all staff, students and the wider school community. Retrieval practice should become part of the shared language of learning and talking about prior learning is something all students can and should be doing, both inside and outside of school.

Poetry recitals

After following Andrew Percival on Twitter (@primarypercival) for many years, I was familiar with the work he had been carrying out with his colleagues to promote a knowledge rich curriculum and evidence-informed approach to teaching and learning. I was very lucky to be able to visit Stanley Road Primary School, where Andrew is deputy headteacher. I was dazzled by the outstanding behaviour, enthusiasm towards learning and the impeccable class work evident in the students' workbooks.

One special highlight was to listen to Miss Conway's Year 5 class recite and perform *Invictus* by William Ernest Henley. Miss Conway and the class were using hand gestures throughout the verbal recital, a good strategy to provide cues and prompts. The class spoke clearly and confidently. I was very impressed not only with their recall abilities but also the positivity and enthusiasm all members of the class demonstrated. It is not just Year 5 that does this, it is a strong part of the school community and culture. Every student at Stanley Road Primary School learns four poems by heart each academic year.

The classes at Stanley Road Primary perform their poetry recitals in assemblies for the rest of the school, but in addition to delivering the poem they have been studying that term they also have to recall a poem they learned previously in another year group so it is not forgotten and is still recallable. The poems selected either link to other aspects of the curriculum or are selected because they have been considered by staff as poems that are worth knowing for their own sake. In addition to studying and learning poetry in class the poems are sent home, as families are encouraged to support their children learn them by heart. Not only can students recall poems verbally, they also learn about the content and context of the poem and can discuss that too. It was beautiful to listen to the class recite a poem in unison and do so with pride and enthusiasm.

When approaching this with a class, it is important to explain the context and meaning of the poem. This will naturally help with understanding the content, but understanding the meaning can support memory too. It is a good idea to learn sections of a poem through chunking and this links to the limitations of working memory. A section can be studied and recalled at a time until students can recall it with with ease, but that section should not be neglected to focus on the next, rather the next part should be added on and build on it. Even when mastered, further practice is useful for increased fluency, ease and confidence.

Retrieval practice with special education needs and disabilities (SEND)

SEND is a very broad term and there are books and professional development opportunities dedicated to specifically focusing on supporting learners with SEND. I will be focusing on SEND within the context of retrieval practice, but I am aware that cognition and learning, communication and interaction, social, emotional, and mental health and sensory and physical needs are all connected in a classroom.

In March 2022, the DfE published a SEND review, with the official website noting that it was, 'a response to the widespread recognition that the system is failing to deliver for children, young people and their families.'[84] There is a need for more support, funding and guidance for schools to enable them to provide exceptional outcomes for learners with SEND.

Professor Becky Francis, Chief Executive at the EEF has stressed the importance of high quality education for children with SEND. She writes, 'Pupils with Special Educational Needs and Disability (SEND) have the greatest need for excellent teaching and are entitled to provision that supports achievement at, and enjoyment of, school. The attainment gap between pupils with SEND and their peers is twice as big as the gap between pupils eligible for free school meals and their peers. However, pupils with SEND are also more than twice as likely to be eligible for free school meals.'[85]

84   Department for Education (2022). *Summary of the SEND review: right support, right place, right time*. Available at: https://www.gov.uk/government/publications/send-and-ap-green-paper-responding-to-the-consultation/summary-of-the-send-review-right-support-right-place-right-time

85   Education Endowment Foundation (2020). *Special Educational Needs in Mainstream Schools*. Available at: https://educationendowmentfoundation.org.uk/education-evi-dence/guidance-reports/send

I can recall a specific experience with a parent of a child with SEND, they did not want their child to be taking part in quizzing and retrieval practice every lesson and wanted me to provide an alternative. I thought about this very carefully and asked for advice from colleagues and experts and looked at the available evidence. I was able to explain to the concerned parent that retrieval practice was a low stakes effective teaching and learning strategy and that excluding their child from this could have a negative impact on their learning and further widen the attainment gap.

I took the parental concerns into consideration and regularly communicated the low stakes nature of retrieval tasks to the child in class. Over time the student developed their confidence as they were able to recall more information and do so with greater ease. Retrieval practice does require resilience and perseverance from all involved.

The EEF published a guidance report in 2020 focusing on special education needs in mainstream schools. There is a lot of useful advice and important recommendations but a key message that stood out for me was, 'To a great extent, good teaching for pupils with SEND is good teaching for all.' The research published in the report suggested that teachers should consider emphasising the following teaching strategies for students with SEND:

- Flexible grouping.
- Cognitive and metacognitive strategies.
- Explicit instruction.
- Using technology to support pupils with SEND.
- Scaffolding.

The use of retrieval cues is also very important for students with SEND, and can be differentiated just as any scaffolding can be increased or decreased as required. The report added, 'Supporting pupils with special educational needs should be part of a proactive approach to supporting all pupils – it is not an "add on". It means understanding the specific barriers pupils face to learning and what they need in order to thrive so that they can be included in all that the school has to offer.'[86] Retrieval practice is certainly a teaching and learning strategy for all learners.

---

86   Education Endowment Foundation (2020). *Special Educational Needs in Mainstream Schools*. Available at: https://educationendowmentfoundation.org.uk/education-evidence/guidance-reports/send

I wish I had more answers and advice to offer in this section. The guidance provided has been shared with me by experts in SEND who have years of experience and expertise, and where there are gaps in the evidence from research their unique knowledge and insight can provide answers and advice. I am very grateful for their support both with my classroom teaching and educational books.

Students with ADHD are more likely than their peers to encounter academic difficulties, inside and outside of the classroom. They can struggle to keep up with the pace in a lesson and maintain focus, although this is not true of all learners with ADHD. In August 2020, there was a research journal published entitled *How much do college students with ADHD benefit from retrieval practice when learning key-term definitions?* The main findings of this study concluded that 'Undergraduate students with ADHD may benefit from retrieval practice but may have difficulty using this strategy consistently'.[87] After carrying out various testing to find out whether students with ADHD benefitted as much as non-ADHD students from self-regulated retrieval practice the results showed that, 'Recall and recognition were as high for students with ADHD as those without ADHD, regardless of whether students regulated their learning or were forced to achieve criterion. Among those who regulated their learning, students with and without ADHD used retrieval practice and feedback to a similar degree. Results support recommending retrieval practice to criterion for college students with and without ADHD.' While this is useful, once again the focus is not on younger learners at primary school.

As shown, there has been research published about retrieval practice and SEND learners but this is a field where further research needs to be conducted. Much more discovery and discussion should be carried out to further support students with special educational needs, disabilities and difficulties at primary age.

In my previous book, *Retrieval Practice 2: Implementing, Embedding and Reflecting*, I included some key quotes from my discussions about retrieval practice with SEND expert Jules Daulby. I feel this is worth repeating and sharing again. Jules explained that 'many retrieval and interleaving strategies are great for children with SEND. But they may not retain it long-term'. This is why repeated retrieval with prompts,

---

87 Knouse, L., Rawson, K. and Dunlosky, J. (2020). How much do college students with ADHD benefit from retrieval practice when learning key-term definitions? *Learning and Instruction*. 68. (8):101330.

cues and scaffolding are so important. Jules added, 'From experience most can do retrieval but they lose the information quicker.' It helps if students with SEND have information encoded through stories, rhymes, say it, hear it and see it with multi-sensory experiences and lots of visual prompts. Jules is an advocate for having high but realistic expectations with SEND students.

Below is a list of recommendations for using retrieval practice in the primary classroom with students with SEND. This list is based on a combination of classroom experience, expertise of others and published evidence.

Establish retrieval practice as a classroom routine

When retrieval practice becomes embedded across a curriculum and accepted by students as part of their daily routine it normalises recall for them. Explain clearly to students that retrieval tasks support their learning, and are low stakes strategies to help them, not assess them.

Regular retrieval practice removes the shock factor of, for example having a pop quiz sprung upon students much to their alarm. A good idea is to openly tell students that next lesson or tomorrow there will be a retrieval quiz on a specific topic. This further reduces the stakes and removes the surprise element, thus giving students the opportunity to prepare for the retrieval quiz should they wish to do so. Students will eventually come to expect to carry out a retrieval task in the lesson as it becomes the norm.

Remove question or countdown timers

There are many online tools and websites for quizzing in the classroom. Be sure to find a quizzing platform that enables you to remove and/or amend the question timer and leader board features.

There are many issues with question timers, but I will focus on just one; that a timer can encourage students to rush to answer questions. In their haste, they may not read the questions or options carefully and make mistakes that do not accurately reflect what they can or cannot recall. Not reading questions carefully can develop into a bad habit that should be avoided.

Instead, sufficient time should be provided for students to read and understand the question, and then recall the answer. How long it will take students to recall information from long-term memory will depend on retrieval strength (how accessible and retrievable information is) and a wide range of factors such as age or complexity of the material and task. This can fluctuate from quick and confident recall to a slower response; the frustrating tip-of-the-tongue moment because retrieval strength is low.

Remove leader boards

Leader boards can motivate some students to compete with their peers, but the priority should instead be to encourage students to focus on their personal bests and closing the specific gaps in their knowledge and recall. It can be demoralising when the same small group of students dominate the leader board. Context is key and there could be a class or occasion where this is appropriate, but most online quizzing tools don't have this feature or if they do they allow teachers to remove it.

Provide retrieval cues as support

Some students with SEND need retrieval cues to allow them to access and understand retrieval practice tasks and questions as well as to support them with the act of recall, either verbal or written. The cues, as discussed previously, can be images, key terms, sentence starters or verbal prompts from the teacher.

Be mindful of the language used

Students with SEND can find the act of retrieval and quizzing high stakes but there are ways teachers can ensure that students can distinguish between low stakes retrieval practice and high stakes, formal summative assessment. When discussing retrieval practice with author and creator of retrievalpractice.org Professor Pooja K. Agarwal, she informed me that she never uses the term 'testing' when it comes to retrieval practice with students (although in research retrieval practice is often referred to as the 'testing effect') because immediately the use of the word 'test' can make it seem high stakes.[88]

Provide opportunities for both verbal and written retrieval practice

There can be students who are reluctant to speak openly and publicly in front of their peers due to a lack of confidence or fear about how their answer or response will be received. This is why building relationships is absolutely crucial and connected to all aspects of teaching and learning in the classroom; to help create a safe and inclusive classroom for all.

---

88   Teacher Talk Radio interview, 6 August 2021. Available at: https://player.fm/series/teachers-talk-radio/the-breakfast-show-with-kate-jones-060821

Promote and provide opportunities for retrieval success

It is important to consider both retrieval success and retrieval challenge when designing retrieval tasks and questions. Barak Rosenshine suggested that, based on research findings, the optimal success rate for fostering student achievement is about 80%. This percentage illustrates that students are learning material as they can recall it, but they are also being challenged. Carefully consider the level of challenge and ensure the questions are desirably difficult but with opportunities for retrieval success. Answering questions correctly and recalling information during a retrieval task can be rewarding, satisfying and motivating, further reducing students' stress. We want our students to embrace and welcome retrieval practice both inside and outside of the classroom.

Provide low stakes feedback

Self- and peer-assessment are not only workload-friendly for the teacher (although teacher supervision and guidance is required), they also offer a low stakes element: they reinforce the idea that retrieval tasks are to improve student learning, not to record assessment data. Students can feel a greater sense of control when marking their own answers, and gain an awareness of their strengths and gaps in knowledge.

No stakes retrieval practice

Another way to conduct a no stakes task is through anonymity. There are online tools such as Mentimeter.com that do not require students to input their name; a code is provided by the teacher for students to enter on the website, they will then see the questions and submit their answers.

Anonymous no stakes quizzing and tasks can at times be frustrating for both student and teacher. The teacher doesn't know who the responses belong to (unless they specifically ask) and the student may want their teacher to know what their answer is, especially if they are proud of their recall response. Despite this limitation no stakes retrieval can still be useful in providing a snapshot overview of the class.

Another way to anonymise retrieval tasks is to instruct students to use a quiz name; a fictional character for example. I did this with my Year 7 class where everyone had a quiz name that had to be a character from Harry Potter. It was very funny with Dumbledore competing against Hagrid but despite the comical element students were still focused and recalling information. The anonymity reduces or can even remove any stress associated with quizzing.

As students progress through school the stakes do increase, from SATS to GCSEs, A-Levels or Highers and then further education. Primary education is a special and joyous – as well as important – period in the development and learning of all children. No one in the school community, from staff and families to the students themselves, want learning to be stressful, intense and high stakes.

The low stakes element of retrieval practice can be tricky to get right, as we don't want students to show apathy or not invest any effort, but it is a vital element to ensure effective retrieval practice becomes embedded across the curriculum and embraced by students. The teacher needs to find a way to communicate the low stakes nature of retrieval practice to their students, while also still holding them to account. Students won't be graded or formally assessed but they are still expected to try hard, concentrate and invest effort into the retrieval tasks.

If unsure whether the retrieval tasks are viewed as high stakes, the easiest way to find out is by asking students and listening to them. Lots of conversations and dialogue about what retrieval practice is and why it helps can make a big difference to lowering the stakes. A teacher cannot say retrieval practice is low stakes but then refer to a specific retrieval practice task on a report sent home, as that can break the trust of the student; reporting formally on a retrieval exercise automatically increases the stakes from low to high.

The low stakes aspect of retrieval practice is mentioned and discussed throughout this book, not just in regard to learners with SEND, but in ensuring retrieval practice is low stakes for all learners. It has been well established through research that, 'acute stress impairs memory retrieval.'[89] Therefore retrieval practice has the potential to be a vicious circle of stress if the low stakes nature is not made clear. Students can become anxious about retrieval tasks and that can have a negative impact on their ability to recall, leading to them not performing well or as well as they hoped, which can then cause further upset, disappointment and stress.

Various studies have shown that regular retrieval practice can reduce stress and anxiety and boost confidence. The study *Classroom-based*

---

89   Smith, A. M., Floerke, V. A. and Thomas, A. K. (2016). Retrieval practice protects memory against acute stress. *Science 354*, 1046–1048.

programs of retrieval practice reduce middle school and high school students' test anxiety[90] involved a survey of 1408 middle school (age 11) and high school students, examining their study strategy preferences and their reactions to in-class retrieval practice. The results showed that in classes where retrieval practice occurred, 92% of students reported that it helped them learn. Of those students asked, 72% reported that retrieval practice made them less nervous for unit tests and exams. This is positive, but 6% of students reported that retrieval practice made them more anxious, although this is a small percentage in comparison, it would be still worth investigating within the class to ensure no learners feel additional stress or pressure.

This study was the first to consider and examine the relationship between retrieval practice and classroom test anxiety. In 2016, Amy M. Smith, Victoria A. Floerkand and Ayanna K. Thomas published *Retrieval practice protects memory against acute stress*.[91] They concluded, 'Thus, we argue that stress may not impair memory retrieval when stronger memory representations are created during encoding. Future research should be geared toward determining the cognitive mechanism by which retrieval practice protects memory against stress. The results of this line of research have the potential to fundamentally transform the way that researchers have viewed the relationship between stress and memory.' Hopefully research will be conducted with younger learners, but this is still something for teachers to be mindful of when conducting regular retrieval practice.

The main message I wish to share with regard to retrieval practice and SEND is that we should be using this strategy with all learners. To not involve students in retrieval practice tasks is to deny them powerful opportunities to learn and make progress, further increasing a disadvantage gap. Teachers need to persist with retrieval practice with learners with SEND, and there are things that can be done and taken into consideration to support these students.

90   Agarwal, P., D'antonio, L., Roediger, H., McDermott, K. and Mcdaniel, M. (2014). Classroom-based programs of retrieval practice reduce middle school and high school students' test anxiety. *Journal of Applied Research in Memory and Cognition*. 3. 10.1016.

91   Smith, A. M., Floerke, V. A. and Thomas, A. K. (2016). Retrieval practice protects memory against acute stress. *Science 354*, 1046–1048.

Retrieval practice placemat

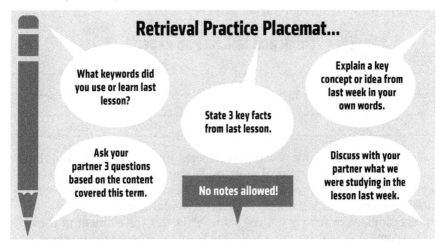

The placemat above is generic and can be used with different ages and subjects or it can be adapted to be more specific. It can be a placemat placed on tables or projected onto the screen for the class to see. The aim of the retrieval practice placemat is to promote verbal discussions among peers about previous content covered and of course retrieve that information from memory by doing so. As the questions are generic this removes subject specific cues and prompts to make it more effortful and challenging.

Think and talk like an expert

The aim of this task is to provide prompts for students when recalling information verbally and encourage them to use subject specific vocabulary (it can also be adapted to think and write like an expert). This might be the key terms included in a knowledge organiser, with students being given opportunities to verbally recall them as well as through written tasks and quizzes, as in the example below from a computing lesson.

You and your partner have five minutes to talk about our topic. Aim to include the following key terms when you are talking so that you think and talk like an expert!

 Think and talk like an expert!

Abstraction	Algorithm	Bug
Data	Decompose	Loop
Key features	Predict	Debug

I would like to see more research conducted into the benefits and the limitations of verbal retrieval practice. Discussion has always played a key role in classrooms and during the pandemic when the classroom became virtual and learning went online, verbal discussions and interactions were simply not the same. This was the element of the classroom I missed the most and I know many others felt the same, both teachers and students.

Students should be asking questions, answering questions and sharing their thoughts, feelings, opinions, ideas and knowledge through verbal and written opportunities. In order for students to learn from one another they have to listen to each other as well as listening to the teacher. Speaking and listening go hand in hand and students, especially younger learners, need explicit guidance and instruction as to how to become effective communicators and articulate their learning verbally both inside and outside of the classroom.

Further recommended reading

Don't Call it Literacy! What every teacher needs to know about speaking, listening, reading and writing. Geoff Barton. (2012)

How to explain absolutely anything to absolutely anyone: The art and science of teacher explanation. Andy Tharby. (2018)

The Inclusive Classroom: A new approach to differentiation. Daniel Sobel and Sara Alston. (2021)

The researchED Guide to Special Educational Needs. Edited by Karen Wespieser. (2021)

CHAPTER 7
VOCABULARY

If ever there was any doubt that retrieval practice is not applicable to all subjects and key stages, vocabulary instruction and recall counteracts that. Every subject and topic will contain vocabulary that students need to be able to understand, recall and use with accuracy. The EYFS *Statutory Framework* states that students are expected to 'use and understand recently introduced vocabulary during discussions about stories, non-fiction, rhymes and poems and during role-play'.[92] Children begin to develop their vocabulary from the moment they start speaking and interacting through verbal communication, and encoding and retrieval are key aspects to vocabulary instruction. Students need to possess and be able to appropriately apply a wide vocabulary to be able to understand and access the curriculum.

Defining key terms with a polished dictionary definition is not enough and the use of dictionaries without further guidance, support and instruction can lead to confusion and misunderstanding. Students need to be able to identify, recognise and understand key vocabulary when it is placed in context. They need to be able to spell key terms and use them with ease, efficiency and confidence in their written work. Students also need to be able to pronounce key terms and use them correctly in their verbal responses.

There has been a lot of excellent evidence-informed literature published in recent years about vocabulary instruction, and there are many key components to it. My suggestions for further reading can be found at the end of this chapter. Alex Quigley has written extensively about closing the vocabulary gap and the importance of this in schools. He writes, 'It is a truth universally acknowledged, that vocabulary knowledge is crucial for pupils' school success. Pupils are language sponges, learning thousands of words each year. Like increases in a child's height, it is a slow but inexorable development. On a daily basis it is near-imperceptible, but when you begin to count the passing of

---

92 Department for Education (2021). *Statutory framework for the early years foundation stage*. DfE. Available at: https://assets.publishing.service.gov.uk/government/uploads/system/uploads/attachment_data/file/974907/EYFS_framework_-_March_2021.pdf

school terms, you can see significant differences occurring.'[93] The authors of *Bringing Words to Life – Robust Vocabulary Instruction*, Isabel L. Beck, Margaret G. McKeown and Linda Kucan write, 'It is clear that a large and rich vocabulary is the hallmark of an educated individual.'[94]

The three-tier model of vocabulary designed by Beck, McKeown and Kucan has become very well known in education; it is very useful and is explored more fully in their book. The concept is that vocabulary can be categorised into one of the three tiers, this is designed to illustrate which words require specific instruction and attention, as shown in the diagram below.

The three-tier model of vocabulary instruction

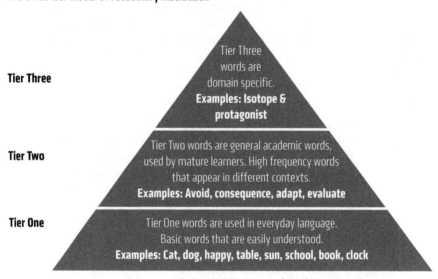

Beck, McKeown & Kucan (2002)

The curse of knowledge is a cognitive bias where we assume that other people know the things we do, or that they have the background to grasp what we are discussing. This is something teachers should be aware of as some students can easily become confused when we use sophisticated or advanced subject specific terminology without

---

93 Quigley, A. (2021). Three pillars of vocabulary teaching. *The confident teacher.* Available at: https://www.theconfidentteacher.com/2021/05/three-pillars-of-vocabulary-teaching/

94 Beck, I. L., McKeown, M. G. and Kucan, L. (2002). *Bringing Words to Life – Robust Vocabulary Instruction.* New York: Guilford Press.

exploring and explaining these key words in the correct context first. Hence why explicit vocabulary instruction is necessary in every classroom.

Receptive vocabulary consists of words that students recognise, know and understand when they hear them. **Expressive vocabulary** includes words that students are able to use confidently when they speak or write. As children progress through school it is expected that both receptive and expressive vocabulary expand and develop.

Teachers play a vital role in developing the vocabulary of learners, as do the family at home. There are words that students will pick up naturally from their surroundings and environment. Children are regularly introduced to new vocabulary from exposure to films, television, social media and, obviously, through reading books. Unfortunately, encountering words naturally does not always secure a strong grasp and understanding of vocabulary, which is why checking for understanding, promoting opportunities to use vocabulary, and regular retrieval practice are all necessary.

Quigley refers to the following as the three key pillars of vocabulary instruction:

1. **Explicit vocabulary teaching** - This involves choosing vocabulary to be learned and building that into curriculum design and delivery. This would link to step one in the five-step curriculum design plan, focusing on essentials.

2. **Incidental vocabulary learning** - This involves providing opportunities for students to be exposed to vocabulary outside the terms selected for explicit vocabulary instruction. Quigley notes: 'You cannot explicitly teach all the words! With over a million words in the English language, teachers make careful selections regarding subject specific vocabulary and those sophisticated Tier 2 words. It is clear that reading rich texts, both in the classroom and beyond the school gates, is critical for language and vocabulary development. Put simply, the more words you read, the more you learn.'

3. **Cultivating word consciousness** - This refers to an awareness of and interest in words and their meaning, context and history. Quigley writes, 'The teaching of word parts (morphology) and word histories (etymology) are some of most well-evidenced methods of explicit vocabulary teaching, but done well, we hand over the baton to our pupils and they become 'word conscious', spying word parts and word families each time they read, talk and write. Faced with

a complex word like 'oligarchy', pupils can recognise the familiar root '-archy', meaning 'rulership'. It offers an essential hook to understand the word, offering more familiar related words like 'monarchy.'[95]

The EEF have published guidance reports focusing on literacy for early years and key stages 1 and 2. The report focusing on improving literacy in KS2 advises teachers to, 'Extend pupils' vocabulary by explicitly teaching new words, providing repeated exposure to new words, and providing opportunities for pupils to use new words.'[96] Retrieval opportunities and tasks can be used to support this.

The report also adds, 'The explicit teaching of new vocabulary should not be seen as an isolated activity. To help pupils to retain and use new vocabulary, teachers should focus on providing pupils with repeated exposure to new vocabulary, including modelling and scaffolding of its use. Repeated exposure to new vocabulary also helps to build pupils' understanding of how new words can be used in different contexts.' This also links with students being able to encode and understand, retrieve, apply and transfer vocabulary across a range of contexts.

It is important that retrieval practice tasks focusing on vocabulary are carried out after vocabulary instruction, discussion and checking for understanding has taken place. The amount of vocabulary students need to learn across all subjects can be overwhelming, but there are strategies to overcome this which include making connections and links between words, repetition of terms and plentiful reading and discussion in class.

Retrieval practice tasks focusing on vocabulary

A lot of online vocabulary tasks for younger children involve word searches, which although they may be popular with some students, are very limited in terms of supporting vocabulary instruction. There are much more effective tasks to do in the class and teachers need to use lesson time wisely, efficiently and effectively. Another idea that is often promoted but can be problematic is asking students to find dictionary definitions and copy them down, again this does not secure deep or

---

95   Quigley, A. (2021). Three pillars of vocabulary teaching. *The confident teacher*. Available at: https://www.theconfidentteacher.com/2021/05/three-pillars-of-vocabulary-teaching/

96   Education Endowment Foundation (2021). *Improving Literacy in Key Stage 2*. Available at: https://educationendowmentfoundation.org.uk/education-evidence/guidance-reports/literacy-ks2

meaningful learning as students can copy text with minimal effort, attention and understanding of the term.

As discussed in chapter 1 with the keyword spotlight task, vocabulary tasks can be conducted at the encoding or retrieval stage, depending on whether the teacher is checking for performance and understanding or long-term recall and learning. A different version of the keyword spotlight is a grid which allows the focus to be extended to more than one key term.

Keyword Spotlight Grid

Keyword	Definition	Use the term correctly in a sentence	Create a question where the keyword is the answer	Draw a picture where the keyword is the answer	Other keywords linked to the keyword

Another example of a task that can be used at the encoding and retrieval stages with vocabulary is the well known Frayer Model originally created by Dorothy Frayer and her colleagues at the University of Wisconsin. This is a graphic organiser which can be easily adapted and used across various subjects with different tier two or three terms.

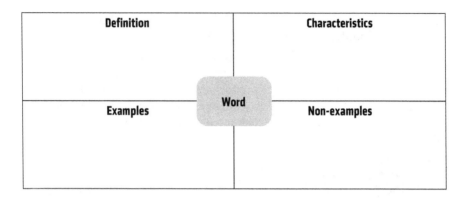

What's the word?

In this game the teacher will provide clues about or definitions of a word, either verbally or shown on the board or a worksheet. Further clues can be shared, and students have to solve what the word is, as shown in the example below. This is a good activity with mini white boards or can be done as a quick quiz. If students use a mini white board they can raise their hand when they know the word and have written it down so other students can't copy or look. An example:

Clue 1. People that were removed from a dangerous threat to safety during the war.

Clue 2. This word describes children that had to leave their homes during World War 2.

Clue 3. This is the term used for a child that was evacuated for safety reasons during the war from cities to the countryside.

Another idea would be to flip this task, providing the word 'evacuee' to students and asking them to provide the clues or definitions.

Connecting clouds with vocabulary

The aim of this task is for students to recall key words linked to a topic and provide a description or definition. The number of clouds can be altered and to differentiate some words or meanings can be provided, or alternatively like the example below, only the first term provided. In this example students will have to fill in the clouds with words that connect to Buddhism. They must also include an accompanying sentence to ensure they can recall meaning.

Vocabulary ... Connecting Clouds

It can be helpful to show a completed example (as shown below) to the class when explaining how this task works. After the task has been completed by students independently, the teacher can cold call and ask students to share their answers with the rest of the class. It can be a good time to use, 'what's your best answer?' Students can be reminded to think about key terms on their knowledge organiser but as it is a retrieval task, they can't look for words to include, but have to recall them. I really enjoyed doing this task with my students because I noticed that different members of the class had included different key terms, but all were relevant and connected to the topic. For younger classes, this can be done verbally and also combined with think-pair-share.

Vocabulary ... Connecting Clouds

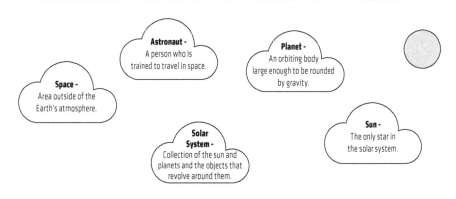

Case study from Ceridwen Eccles about using retrieval practice to support vocabulary in the primary classroom.

Ceridwen Eccles is another evidence-informed teacher that I follow and learn from via social media. Through sharing creative and innovative ideas as well as her open and honest reflections, Ceridwen has gained a large following on Twitter @Teacherglitter. I have often thought; I wish Ceridwen was my teacher because her lessons seem so wonderful. I don't think there is a greater compliment we can give to a teacher than that.

Ceridwen is passionate about using retrieval practice in the classroom and here she shares how she has done so with a focus on vocabulary.

Over the last few years, I have embedded retrieval practice as a standard expectation in all the curriculum areas I teach, and feel the benefit to improving retention and expansion of knowledge and skills of the learners is intrinsically linked. One of the biggest caveats I have over the application of retrieval practice is that it doesn't overshadow the delivery of that knowledge and doesn't become a 'tag on' without purpose. For me, retrieval practice becomes a purposeful, successful tool within your teaching tool box when it is coupled with careful thought of how knowledge is taught, with regards to cognitive overload, and what you want the knowledge to build and enhance further down the line. You cannot possibly expect a learner to recall information if they were unable to encode it in the first place.

This is an area I hold at the forefront of my planning, particularly when I am looking at vocabulary retrieval. I hold a model (in my head) that takes into account how I teach the vocabulary, how I ensure the vocabulary is successfully encoded and transferred into the long-term memory and how it can be independently applied.

Each of these three steps is reliant on the step before, as shown here:

Explicit teaching of vocabulary takes the same format whether it is vocabulary I want them to learn as part of a science lesson or whether it is learning new words in context from a class read to use within their writing.

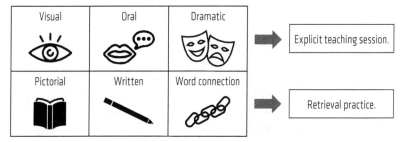

I create cards that can be displayed that have a visual representation of the word, the meaning, synonyms and the words in context. When using a class read, I select words that will fit with my model and ensure the ones I am introducing will enhance comprehension and can be ones that they would use in their own writing. Once I have presented the cards, I instruct students to repeat the words after me. Students repeat the word using different voices. Play with the sounds in their mouth. They will then have opportunities to create an action too.

Another useful tool is for students to play with the synonyms of that word in context or to replace the word with the definition so they can think about the power and effect that specific words have on the flow of a sentence and why an author might have selected the words they have. This not only creates a richer understanding of the word you wish them to remember, it will also feed it into the application of the word at an independent level. An example of how I would scaffold this can be seen in the example below:

frantically:

Adverb

Move in an over-excited, crazy way due to excitment or fear.

Synonyms:

Wild, crazy, frenzied.

"High above the sea was a huge black raven frantically beating it's wings against the wind and rain."

'High above the sea was a huge black raven *moving in an over-excited crazy way*, beating its wings against the wind and the rain. It whirled upwards, then vanished back into the night.'

Read the passage and try changing the bold definition each time with the words wildly, crazily and frenziedly.

We came across the word **frantically** in Nevermoor when Hawthorn was waving his torch at the zombies frantically. Have you heard the word anywhere else?

Create an action for the word frantically and say the word as you perform it.

I think it is important to share with the children why you are doing retrieval practice so they become invested and indeed make suggestions of words they want to include that they may be struggling with. I liken it to eating something delicious that we don't want to forget the flavour of. This always makes my students laugh and we have conversations around what juicy and tasty words I am going to get them to eat today!

Literacy recall activity 11/02/2020 $\frac{7}{7}$

1. Use the word odious in a sentence

   Baz Charlton, who is Noelle's horrible, odious patron, took another large swig of brandy from a bottle. ✓ ①

2. Describe what the word gullible means

   The word gullible means that you believe anything someone tells you, your cat just swam breaststroke and you believed it.✓ ①

3. Draw a picture for the word **engrossed**

   ✓ ①

During retrieval practice, the children will have opportunities to draw their own visual representation, write the word in context and show synonyms. This takes the form of a daily low stakes quiz on a range of vocabulary taught from that academic year, individual word exploration using the Freyer model, matching games, and oral paired work.

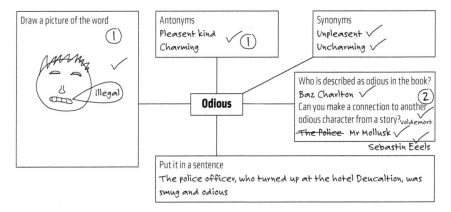

The application of these words within independent work is proof that the vocabulary has been successfully encoded and retained, this is also demonstrated when weeks later a word I have taught them is being used accurately in context. Another indication of success is when links and connections can be made with words and etymology across subjects and when the children can make comparisons with words they have been taught and think of excellent synonyms of their own. I think it is important to make sure vocabulary explicitly taught is recorded so that children will continue to use and retain their vocabulary learning from previous year groups and the next teacher is aware of the vocabulary they should expect to see within the writing of their new class.

Thank you to Ceridwen Eccles for sharing her knowledge, experiences and enthusiasm about retrieval practice in the primary classroom to support vocabulary instruction. Follow Ceridwen on Twitter @TeacherGlitter and visit her teaching and learning blog https://teacherglitter.wordpress.com/.

Go for gold

The example shown is a 'go for gold' task based on the KS2 topic 'Mountains'. Students have to recall from memory what they can about mountains and should aim to include as many of the words listed below as possible. The words also act as retrieval cues to direct students to specific target memories.

GO FOR GOLD

Bronze: Mountains | Tourism | Valley

Silver: Summit | Range | Ridge

Gold: Tectonic Plates | Altitude | Climate

I created this resource to encourage my students to use subject specific vocabulary in their written answers. Once again this can be used as a consolidation task or retrieval task, depending on when it is used in the learning process. Go for gold is similar to 'think and talk like an expert' but this task strikes a balance between retrieval success and retrieval challenge.

The words in the bronze category should be words that every single member of the class can include, therefore everyone has a taste of success and a boost of confidence and motivation. The words in silver and gold are more challenging, but every member of the class is being challenged, not just a targeted group of those considered 'more able'. This task includes support for all and challenge for all with every student encouraged to go for gold. Younger students may struggle to access this but it can be adapted by reducing the number of key terms or be used as a verbal retrieval practice task.

Vocabulary games for retrieval practice

Games in the classroom can lead to a mixed reaction, as there are some games which are fun and enjoyable for students but provide little if any learning opportunities. This is a waste of precious lesson time, but I do believe retrieval practice can be engaging as well as effective. All the games and tasks shared here have been used in my classroom with the explicit focus and purpose being retrieval practice.

Keyword grids

Weather	Climate	Tropical
Equator	Humidity	Latitude
Longitude	Precipitation	Biome

A simple task that is very versatile as there are many ways to use it in the classroom. Some suggested ideas include:

■ Define each word.

■ Explain how the keywords link.

■ Write an answer and aim to include all the following terms – either a sentence for each keyword or a paragraph including as many as possible.

■ If the keyword is the answer, what is the question?

The teacher can model pronunciation of keywords and this can also support spelling. Students can create their own keywords grid, they are simply given a blank grid and write down keywords from memory linked to the topic. This can be a way of including vocabulary from a knowledge organiser.

It can be used in the study of languages as shown below with different words in Welsh linked to the topic of school – Ysgol. The words can be translated, or combined to write a sentence or paragraph, or used to prompt a verbal conversation. To provide further support images can be added as retrieval cues but it is worth being mindful of cue overload; that too many cues can make the retrieval redundant as it becomes too easy with too much support.

Ysgol	Chwaraeon	Mathemateg
Gwisg Ysgol	Llyfrau	Ffrindiau
Gwyddoniaeth	Celf	Athro

Vocabulary chase

Board games in the classroom are a contentious subject, but I think their effectiveness depends on the purpose and design of both the task and questions asked. This is a straightforward game I created with a blank template where again the focus is on subject specific keywords. Dice and counters are required to play 'vocabulary chase'. Students roll the dice and based on the number, move their counter to that box. Each box has a keyword inside. The boxes are colour coded with the instructions as follows:

Yellow = Use the word correctly in a sentence.

Red = Give a definition.

Blue = Follow the instructions.

Alternatively, to save on colour printer ink the colours can be replaced with shapes, so 'Use the word correctly in a sentence' becomes a square, and so on. This game can be played during the middle of the topic or unit to check for understanding and as part of consolidation, or alternatively once some time has passed and without any support, for retrieval practice. Students could create their own as long as they include relevant and related key terms. The example below is from my classroom with older students but I think it could be adapted and used in the primary classroom. If you do create your own version of this or any of the resources please do let me know and share.

Vocabulary Chase

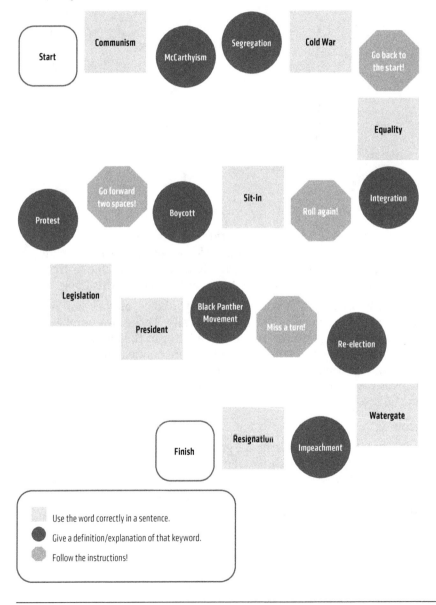

Start

Communism

McCarthyism

Segregation

Cold War

Go back to the start!

Equality

Go forward two spaces!

Sit-in

Integration

Protest

Boycott

Roll again!

Legislation

President

Black Panther Movement

Miss a turn!

Re-election

Watergate

Finish

Resignation

Impeachment

Use the word correctly in a sentence.

Give a definition/explanation of that keyword.

Follow the instructions!

6x6 vocabulary grid

Roll a pair of dice and come up with keywords connected to our topic beginning with...

	1	2	3	4	5	6
6	A	J	I	D	F	B
5	H	K	B	W	R	I
4	Y	J	O	F	S	U
3	L	C	A	M	T	N
2	G	O	V	P	C	D
1	R	Z	S	E	S	T

This is the main way I use the 6x6 grid with my classes. Again, a pair of dice are required but the same grid can be used across a wide range of ages, subjects and topics. This template is available to freely download and use, the link can be found at the back of this book.

In pairs or small groups, students roll a pair of dice, as they will need a number to use both vertically and horizontally. Those two numbers will lead students to a square where there is a letter of the alphabet. Using that letter they have to say out loud a keyword connected to the topic or learning intention, alternatively they can write this down as a record of the words they have recalled. Then their partner rolls and does the same and so on.

Scrabble

This is a twist on the classic board game (although not always well known to younger students!). Students have to recall key words linked to a topic. As they write each word they have to use basic numeracy skills to calculate its scrabble score. The aim can be to think of as many words as possible or to find the highest scoring word.

A_1 B_3 C_3 D_2 E_1 F_4

G_2 H_4 I_1 J_8 K_5 L_1

M_3 N_1 O_1 P_3 Q_{10} R_1

S_1 T_1 U_1 V_4 W_4 X_8

Y_4 Z_{10}

These can also be created for other languages; I made a Welsh version to use with my classes that can also be freely downloaded.

A_1 B_3 C_3 Ch_4 D_2

Dd_2 E_1 F_4 Ff_5 G_2

Ng_5 H_4 I_1 J_8 L_1

Ll_8 M_3 N_1 O_1 P_3

Ph_{10} R_1 Rh_4 S_1 T_1

Th_{10} U_3 W_4 Y_8

Freerice.com

This website freerice.com has two key aims. Firstly, to support students develop their range of vocabulary and understanding and secondly, fight against global hunger. Their website states, 'Freerice is an educational trivia game that helps you get smarter while making a difference for people around the world. Every question you answer correctly raises 10 grains of rice for the World Food Programme (WFP) to support its work saving and changing lives around the world.'

Freerice is a literacy game where a single word will be shown and four words will be provided as answers, with only one word representing the correct meaning. Students have to click on the correct definition:

ferocious means:

weary

exhausted

fierce

central

Students click on an answer and are informed instantly if they are correct or not. As students progress through higher levels, the words become more challenging. For every correct answer the World Food Programme donates ten grains of rice to help end hunger. Students can create an account that they can return to and login if they wish to track their results (there is also a global scoreboard for those who are competitive). Freerice is also available as an app.

Freerice.com also has different categories and subjects to select from including history, capitals and countries of the world and much more including languages with Spanish, French and Latin. There is an option to control the difficulty level from easiest to hardest. The teacher cannot upload the questions so the other categories and subjects outside of vocabulary are not always appropriate for primary learners. Freerice. com is an opportunity to practise and expand vocabulary.

Mentimeter

The website www.mentimeter.com can be used for presentations and quizzing. Mentimeter.com is workload and user friendly and the anonymity for students ensures low/no stakes. There are different ways it can be used for retrieval practice including open ended and multiple choice questions, so it can be used for cued or free recall.

The word cloud option can be used for vocabulary, it is a no stakes option as students respond anonymously. This has pros and cons and for that reason I use mentimeter in conjunction with other online quizzing tools. For the word cloud option, a question is asked and students can only answer using single words, but they can submit between one and ten depending how many the teacher will allow. Words become larger when they are entered multiple times.

Example 1: Students had to recall synonyms for the word 'nice'.

Nice

Example 2: Students used different adjectives to describe World War One trenches.

What words would you use to describe WW1 trenches?

Example 3: Students can also elaborate on the vocabulary with an explanation or description.

Describe general life in the WW1 trenches.

dug into the ground where soldiers lived. They were very muddy, uncomfortable and the toilets overflowed. These

It muddy and wet, dirty and boring.

Life was miserable, there were dead bodies everywhere and rats

Life was tough in the WW1 trenches. It was either boring or it could be scary with the thought of going over the top. There were lots of diseases such as Trench foot & lice. It was generally very uncomfortable for soldiers in the trench.

as Trench foot & lice. It was generally very uncomfortable for soldiers in the trench.

living conditions were very bad

Vocabulary instruction is an integral and important element of primary education. Teachers play a crucial role in supporting students' vocabulary development, as do parents and carers. When using strategies to widen a learner's repertoire, we know the approaches are working because we can hear the students using sophisticated vocabulary during peer discussions or when answering a question. Vocabulary will also be used correctly in written responses and answers. Tier three terminology across the different units taught becomes embedded into student vocabulary and students are able to apply and transfer key terms in different contexts. Explanations and answers can become richer with a wider vocabulary, and students become more articulate and confident.

Further recommended reading

Bringing Words to Life: Robust Vocabulary Instruction. Isabel L. Beck, Margaret G. McKeown and Linda Kucan. (2002)

Closing the Vocabulary Gap. Alex Quigley. (2018)

Reading Recharged: Activities to put the spark into guided and whole-class reading. Alex Barton. (2021)

The Art and Science of Teaching Primary Reading. Christopher Such. (2021)

CHAPTER 8
RETRIEVAL PRACTICE ACROSS THE SCHOOL COMMUNITY

As we saw in the introduction to this book, during my conversations and interviews with teachers and school leaders, some of my questions were focused on retrieval practice across the whole school community of staff, students and families.

Q) Have staff and/or students noticed any benefits of retrieval practice?

Q) Have you informed or involved the wider school community (parents, carers and families) with regards to retrieval practice?

This was very interesting as responses varied considerably. The majority of responses demonstrated that teachers and leaders are enthusiastically engaging with research linked to retrieval practice and implementing it across the curriculum and in their lessons. Some schools had begun to explain to the students what retrieval practice was and why they were using quizzing and recall to support learning (as Dyfan from Myddleton College was able to demonstrate).

The majority of schools I spoke to said they had not yet explained the concept and benefits of retrieval practice to parents, carers and families, but some had done so and felt they had successfully managed to encourage students to use retrieval practice at home with their families, who were keen to support their children.

There are many benefits of retrieval practice, some explained by research and others that are clear through classroom experience alone. These benefits are direct and indirect, and academic and pastoral. Below is a summary of what I consider to be the main benefits of retrieval practice inside and outside of the classroom. Everyone should be aware of these, not just teachers and school leaders.

- Retrieval practice is regarded as one of the most effective study strategies to support learning for learners of all ages and across a range of subjects and topics. It can support students with SEND and EAL.

- Testing and quizzing help identify which information a student can recall from memory, as well as gaps in their knowledge. This is useful insight for the teacher, student and their parents and carers.

- Research has shown that regular retrieval practice can lead to better organisation and transfer of knowledge.

- Using retrieval practice in lessons can indirectly encourage students to prepare for quizzes at home and carry out retrieval practice independently, especially with lesson resources such as knowledge organisers or booklets.

- There is evidence (focusing on older students but still positive) that regular retrieval practice in lessons can reduce anxiety and boost confidence when carrying out high stakes assessments.

- Retrieval practice is a low cost and high impact strategy, therefore easy and effective for schools to introduce. It can also be used at home with ease.

- It is a very versatile and flexible strategy. Retrieval tasks, games and quizzes can be highly enjoyable, engaging, fun and rewarding for students. It certainly is not – and should not be – stressful or mundane for them.

There is more to share and focus on other than just the benefits of retrieval practice, such as the research behind it and varying techniques. When I work with schools I often show them the diagrams below to represent the wider school community.

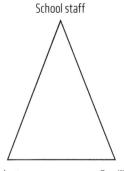

I use the two triangles because there is a distinction between what teaching staff - leaders, teachers and teaching assistants - need to know about retrieval practice, compared to what students and their families need to know. As educators we need to have greater insight, knowledge and understanding because we have to design and deliver a curriculum to students and create tasks and questions that are carefully crafted to enhance teaching, learning and ultimately long-term memory. Students and families should have knowledge of retrieval practice in terms of what it is, what the benefits are and how it can be used, but they do not need the same depth of knowledge as educators in order to use it effectively at home.

Triangle 1: The teaching body

Leaders at all levels

Classroom teachers   Support staff

In terms of the teaching staff, everyone should be aware of retrieval practice and ensure it is used effectively to support students' learning and inform future planning. Retrieval practice can highlight gaps in student knowledge or illustrate misconceptions and this is where teachers can be responsive and plan their future lessons accordingly to address this.

Retrieval practice is a staple teaching and learning strategy. It should be taking place in every classroom, with every child; but this can be easier said than done. To do this, teachers need to understand the research and evidence and gain insight into how students learn and how to design and deliver lessons that support retrieval practice. Teachers also need time to implement and embed retrieval practice in their classroom; the research isn't one size fits all, so needs to be adapted to their unique classroom context. It is important that teachers have time to reflect on how they are using retrieval practice in their lessons at an individual, key stage or whole school level.

When I deliver training to staff on retrieval practice I often encourage teaching assistants (TAs) or learning support assistants (LSAs) to attend too. Support staff in a primary school play an essential role in the progress of students and supporting classroom teachers. It is important and necessary that TAs and LSAs receive professional development enabling them to understand the research behind retrieval practice and how they can further support the learners they work with by using this strategy.

The EEF published a guidance report[97] in 2018 entitled *Making Best Use of Teaching Assistants. Guidance to help primary and secondary schools make the best use of TAs*. The guidance report suggested that schools:

- Use TAs to help students develop independent learning skills and manage their own learning.
- Ensure TAs are fully prepared for their role in the classroom.
- Use TAs to deliver high quality one-to-one and small group support using structured interventions.
- Adopt evidence-based interventions to support TAs in their small group and one-to-one instruction.

Knowledge of the limitations of working memory (with cognitive load theory and models of memory) and the importance of recalling information from long-term memory can be very helpful for classroom staff, as they support students with their learning and progress at both the encoding and retrieval stages of the learning process.

To embed retrieval practice within a school's culture, it must come from the top. It should be passionately promoted, encouraged and led by leaders at all levels. Leaders can, as with all aspects of school leadership, lead by example in terms of their attitude towards retrieval practice. A primary school differs significantly to a secondary context as leaders tend to have more of a teaching timetable, therefore making it very possible to visibly and actively lead by example.

Leaders can also engage with evidence, and share it with their teams and colleagues; this can be achieved through sharing blogs, articles, books, podcasts and more. Leaders should support classroom teachers

---

97 Education Endowment Foundation (2018). *Making best Use of Teaching Assistants*. Available at: https://educationendowmentfoundation.org.uk/education-evidence/guidance-reports/teaching-assistants

to learn more about retrieval practice and put guidance in place with school policies to promote a consistent classroom routine across the school. Leaders play a crucial role in reviewing how teachers are implementing and embedding retrieval practice into their classroom planning and practice. This should be supportive and developmental, not judgmental, as education consultant and trainer Chris Moyse says when he advises leaders to focus on 'improve not prove'.

Triangle 2: The wider school community

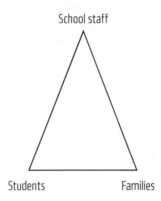

It is vital that students understand why they are being regularly quizzed in lessons, and we can explain this to them in a child friendly way void of any jargon. It can help students if they understand and realise why they are regularly being quizzed. Imagine the worry and stress a child could experience if they misunderstand retrieval practice and think they have to complete high stakes testing every day at school.

The ultimate goal is for students to be able to use retrieval practice techniques outside of the classroom to test themselves, find gaps in their knowledge and then close those gaps with further retrieval practice. Students in KS2 are more likely to do this independently but some will still need support and guidance. For younger children self-testing and quizzing should be carried out at home with support and guidance, this is where the role of parents, carers and families becomes key.

In terms of when to begin dialogue with families, it really is a case of the sooner the better. Conversations between school and families begin when a child starts their learning journey and should be ongoing throughout their school life. Grenier writes, 'Parents are essential partners in children's early learning. Both the home and the early years setting can each do a great deal to support the child. They achieve even more when they work co-operatively together in a respectful partnership.'[98] There are many factors that influence parental engagement but the key aspect is to be resilient and keep the lines of communication as open as possible.

Grenier also warns teachers about unconscious bias, where judgments can be reached unconsciously due to existing stereotypes. He writes, 'Every child and family is unique. It's important not to make negative assumptions about disadvantaged children. Instead of making assumptions, we need to know, value and understand the children we are working with. Many families in disadvantaged circumstances do a great job supporting their children's learning.' It's important that parents and carers understand how influential and helpful they can be with the development, learning and progress of their child.

In terms of where to begin, a basic grasp of cognitive psychology and academic research can be very helpful, but this can easily become overwhelming, especially with new and unfamiliar terminology. Bradley Busch and Edward Watson from InnerDrive work with teachers, students and parents as they recognise the importance of educating and supporting everyone within the school community. Busch and Watson write, 'Educating parents is important. Parents have limited knowledge from a small sample size of what does and doesn't work (ie. their own experiences with their children). Schools and teachers have a wide, varied and deep experience base of helping students achieve educational success. It therefore stands to reason that part of the role and responsibility of a school is to transmit and transfer this knowledge. Parents evenings, evening workshops and newsletters are great ways to communicate this to parents.'[99]

It can be very frustrating for students and teachers when content from lessons is forgotten, but research has helped us learn and understand that forgetting is a friend of learning.[100] Forgetting is an important and natural part of the learning process, and an awareness of this can help

---

98   Grenier, J. (2020). *Working with the revised Early Years Foundation Stage. Principles into Practice.* Sheringham Nursery School and Children's Centre. Available at: http://development-matters.org.uk/wp-content/uploads/2020/10/Working-with-the-revised-Early-Years-Foundation-Stage-Principles-into-Practice-.pdf

99   Busch, B. and Watson, E. (2021). *The Science of Learning: 99 Studies That Every Teacher Needs to Know.* Abingdon: Routledge. Page 27.

100 Bjork, R. A. and Bjork, E. L. (2019). Forgetting as the friend of learning: Implications for teaching and self-regulated learning. *Adv. Physiol. Educ.* 43, 164–167.

us to revisit previous content to interrupt and counteract forgetting. However, students and families aren't often aware of this. It can be demoralising for the child when they forget, and for families when their child forgets information they have been taught in school this can cause panic and alarm. As mentioned, we don't need to share with students and families the in-depth knowledge of cognitive psychology but some of the information about how learning happens should be shared, especially when it comes to forgetting.

Parents should be reassured that if their child can't recall something, then not to worry and that we can overcome this. Students should understand that it's ok and that we all forget, we can share examples and anecdotes of us forgetting – it even happens to teachers!

Retrieval Practice - What do students and parents need to know?

1. A basic overview and introduction to cognitive psychology & key findings from academic research.	2. Explain the various benefits, both direct and indirect of using retrieval practice.	3. Provide & model explicit examples & retrieval strategies such as flash cards, brain dumps etc.	4. Explain the importance of refelction & acting on identified gaps in knowledge.

I have created a document containing an overview of retrieval practice that can be shared with parents, it can be downloaded freely by scanning the QR code at the back of this book. Please do feel free to share it within your wider school community. There is no school branding and it is generic, but if you wish to adapt my version and create your own that is personal to your school and links with your curriculum and/or curriculum intentions, please feel free to do so. When creating this I thought carefully about what parents need to know, what will help them and ultimately help students too.

Below are the contents of the guide I created:

The starting point has to be an explanation of retrieval practice, as many will be unfamiliar with this term although they will recognise that quizzing takes place in school. This is my explanation, which I intended to be concise and helpful (again, please feel free to copy and use or adapt).

What is retrieval practice?

Retrieval practice is a teaching and learning strategy that can be used inside or outside of the classroom to help children learn. Retrieval practice focuses on getting information out of the memory. Through this act of retrieval – which involves recalling information verbally or through writing – that memory is then strengthened. Retrieval practice helps memory and therefore helps to improve learning.

In lessons teachers will regularly quiz their classes on what they have studied previously. This is not a high stakes test or assessment, but instead a way to check what students can or cannot remember and help improve their memory, knowledge and confidence.

There has been a lot of research published that tells us this is an effective strategy for all learners of all ages. The more children practice recalling information from memory, the easier it will be to recall that information in the future.

Secondly, I think it's important to briefly summarise the main benefits of retrieval practice in a way that is very clear and precise.

What are the benefits of retrieval practice?

- It's a powerful strategy to help children learn.
- It identifies where any gaps in knowledge are.
- Regular retrieval practice can boost confidence.
- It can be fun, enjoyable and rewarding!

This can be discussed with families in more depth at a later date but as an introduction it is useful.

Next, it is very important to explain how retrieval practice can be used at home. This has to be communicated to families if we are to hope that retrieval practice will be used outside of school.

How can you use retrieval practice at home with your child or children?

- Ask questions about the content studied in class.
- Ask about key vocabulary and its meaning.
- Ask your child/children to write down from memory as much as they can about a topic or lesson they studied last week; make sure they focus on what they learned, not the tasks they did.
- Ask questions about topics from last term or further back!

If you use flashcards, booklets or knowledge organisers these can also be used to support retrieval practice at home. If families have concerns that regular testing is taking place in school then it is helpful to explicitly explain the key differences between retrieval practice as a low stakes strategy in contrast to high stakes assessment.

Testing has many negative connotations with stress and mental health implications but retrieval practice as we know is a very powerful and effective teaching and learning strategy. Students should be self-testing and quizzing to find out what they can't recall and where the gaps are in their knowledge both inside and outside of the classroom. A child may go home and tell their family that they have been tested a lot in school and this might cause some distress and anger, hence the importance of keeping everyone in the community updated, aware and informed.

How is retrieval practice different from testing/assessments?

- The focus is low stakes; this is very different from testing.
- Quizzes and retrieval tasks are fun, engaging and enjoyable for students.
- Scores and results are not formally recorded.
- Cues and prompts can be provided to offer support.
- Students are clearly told retrieval tasks are not tests or assessments.

To further reassure families that retrieval practice doesn't turn schools into exam factories with constant drilling and testing happening in lessons, a description of what different forms of retrieval practice look like in the classroom can provide clarity.

What are the different types of retrieval practice in the classroom?

- Multiple choice questions and quizzes. These can be done on paper or online.
- Verbal recall – talking about what students can recall.
- Writing from memory about what we have studied.
- Games and play that help children recall information.
- Think, pair and share – students recall information, discuss it with a partner then share their answers with the class.
- Using mini-white boards to write down answers, share with the teacher then erase.

There will likely be some families that are keen to embrace retrieval practice to support their child with their memory, learning and progress. If families do want to find out more then we should encourage this. Below are listed some useful websites – which could be provided as hyperlinks or QR codes – and I have recommended books for parents at the end of this chapter.

Further reading and information about retrieval practice:

■ www.retrievalpractice.org
■ www.learningscientists.org
■ www.innerdrive.co.uk

I worked with a primary school in Manchester that was keen to take retrieval practice to the next level and involve families at home. The school was already sending a weekly newsletter home for each year group, the theme of which was to explain what that year group had been learning about that week, in addition to important notices and updates. This seemed a perfect opportunity to include retrieval practice.

Retrieval practice and the importance of quizzing, forgetting and memory were explained in a newsletter and the ones that followed contained a series of questions and answers for students. The questions were not based on the content taught that week but instead reached further back, either two or three weeks and sometimes even more. The idea was to encourage families to ask their children specific – and useful – questions about what they had learned previously. The answers were provided and advice was given that if the child could not recall the correct answer, to not panic as forgetting is an important part of the learning process, but instead to share the correct answers and then ask again at a later date.

The newsletter was an informal way to introduce families to retrieval practice and encourage quizzing at home. This wasn't a form of homework or home learning but simply a tool to promote retrieval practice, making it part of the wider school community and promoting good learning habits for students while also engaging families. The challenge with this is that naturally some families will be very keen to digest the weekly newsletter and ask questions whereas others may not even read the newsletter. Parental engagement can vary significantly and that does bring challenges.

Parents can become confused when, after observing their child spending time re-reading and highlighting their notes, that child doesn't do as well on an assessment as they hoped. What went wrong? Some study strategies are deemed more effective than others, and it is important that parents understand this. Retrieval practice is regarded as highly effective in contrast to highlighting, re-reading and underlining. If parents are aware of this, they can intervene and encourage their child to use effective strategies.

Parents can get involved with retrieval practice at home through quizzing and using flashcards with their child. Knowing what retrieval practice is and what its benefits are will help parents to understand why their child's teacher regularly quizzes them in lessons. This can also bust some myths and relieve any concerns that parents might have about 'drill and kill' high stakes testing.

There are many benefits of retrieval practice but to use it to its full potential, it needs to become embedded in a school's culture and become part of the language of learning across the wider school community. The best way to achieve this is through sharing and explaining the many benefits of retrieval practice and various techniques with leaders at all levels, classroom teachers, TAs and LSAs, students, parents, carers and families. As someone who has spent years working hard on this, I know it does take time and requires commitment and effort from all in the school community. It is challenging, especially as levels of parental engagement and student motivation vary significantly, but do persevere. It is worth it.

A great example of how parents and carers can actively support retrieval practice is by encouraging the use of flash cards, with a question on one side and the answer on the other. A parent or family member can ask the question on the flashcard and check the answer on the back. No prior subject knowledge is required on the part of the quizzer as the answers are provided to give instant feedback. It is worth putting correct answers in one pile and incorrect – or questions where answers couldn't be recalled – in another pile to revisit. This links in with the previous point about forgetting and that it is part of learning. Retrieval practice (unlike highlighting and re-reading) shows clearly what information and content can be recalled and where the gaps are so revision can focus on that until it does become recallable with further retrieval practice.

Case study: Embedding retrieval practice across the school community at New Horizons primary school by Ella Martin

I have been fortunate to work with staff at Thinking Schools Academy Trust (TSAT). One of their teaching and learning priorities is further developing understanding of memory. As part of the research for this book I had a conversation with Ella Martin, TSAT hub lead for teaching and learning and teacher of Year 6 at New Horizons primary school in Kent. Below Ella explains how TSAT has informed and involved everyone across the Trust with retrieval practice.

At New Horizons School, we introduced retrieval practice as part of our 'Teach to Remember' agenda which was part of our school improvement plan for 2022-2023. This is part of a larger drive, like most schools, to ensure that our curriculum is knowledge rich. We focused particularly on identifying the core knowledge in our curriculum, ensuring knowledge is taught to be remembered and planning vertically and horizontally across year groups and subjects.

When introducing retrieval practice, our focus was firstly on how we could successfully introduce this to teaching staff and TAs before disseminating it to the rest of the staff in school, students and parents.

Introducing retrieval practice to staff

In order to ensure that retrieval practice was incorporated into daily teaching, staff needed to know that retrieval wasn't a new buzzword or craze in education, and there is a wealth of research on the impact of retrieval practice to substantiate this. Working within an academy which does focus on evidence-based teaching was a benefit as many teachers and TAs are comfortable and confident discussing educational research, so I knew it wouldn't overload staff if I included references to research within professional development training. However, not all staff are as confident with educational research and many did not have much prior knowledge of memory. Therefore, the initial training in memory had to accommodate the varying levels of knowledge and understanding.

During the staff training I explained Baddley and Hitch's multi-store model, the limitations of our memory, overcoming the limitations of working memory by considering cognitive load, chunking and dual-coding. This was followed by discussing utilising long-term memory and how to improve retrieval strength. Throughout I kept bringing this back to the classroom, focusing on how to apply our understanding of memory to our daily teaching and curriculum design, and providing staff with practical ideas. Alongside this training, staff were provided with a hand-out recapping some of the core concepts we had discussed within the training, resources and links to further reading, such as Kate's previous books and various blogs and podcasts.

The feedback from this initial training was captured on a Microsoft Forms quiz and demonstrated that staff had gained a lot. A real benefit was that TAs were involved and many of them spoke to me after the session about how they do not often receive this kind of training. They found it interesting and were enthusiastic about how to apply it to their small group teaching and interventions. This made me reflect on how important it is to include TAs in training and develop their understanding of cognitive science.

I wanted to make the most of this thirst for knowledge and enthusiasm from the teachers and TAs so I approached the SLT about the possibility of developing a research library. The SLT agreed and I ordered some fantastic books on retrieval practice and memory. I was already sharing a 'Teaching and Learning Bulletin' fortnightly with staff where I summarise educational research, include links to blogs and articles, and share education news, but I focused purely on memory for a term to keep up the momentum.

Once staff had this basic understanding of retrieval practice and how it linked into the science of memory, we provided further CPD; firstly, on salient knowledge then knowledge banks (this is how we refer to knowledge organisers, as banks of knowledge) and retrieval practice. The focus on salient knowledge was part of wider CPD on a knowledge rich curriculum. I referred to the memory training I had delivered, focusing on the importance of ensuring children encode the knowledge you intend them to. Often children can encode episodic memories such as remembering that a bee flew into the classroom or they were allowed to use coloured pens and sit with their friends, rather than always encoding the semantic memory (the factual knowledge) of the lesson. Therefore, in one CPD session, staff were encouraged to explicitly identify what the salient knowledge was of their lessons for the following week and consider how they would communicate this to the children. With the introduction of knowledge banks, this was easier for staff because the salient knowledge was included on the knowledge bank. Teachers could put a picture of the knowledge bank up on their PowerPoint and direct children to the knowledge they were learning within that lesson. This was followed by a staff meeting focusing on why we use knowledge banks and how to integrate them more within lessons.

Retrieval continued to be a high priority in school as we launched memory-based action research projects. The areas of focus included salient knowledge, purposeful use of knowledge banks, retrieval quizzes and purposeful use of DNAs for retrieval ('do now activities' at the start of lessons). While all staff had received CPD in all these areas and were beginning to incorporate them into their practice, the aim of the action research was to develop champions in these areas who could support colleagues. Teaching staff were able to choose the area they wanted to work on and it was suggested that this could link to one of their personal growth targets. Rather than performance management, we have a model of personal growth where staff chose their own targets for the academic year which they regularly reflect on digitally.

Groups were formed and staff worked together across year groups to share what they were currently doing and come up with a plan for how they would develop their current practice. Time was planned into our CPD timetable for staff to get together in their groups, reflect and feedback, and time was dedicated to discussing their action research in phase meetings.

The 'teaching to remember' agenda was kept a priority within the school and at a Trust level. Multiple times a year, we have MAT-meet events; trust-wide CPD events with keynote speakers. The guest speakers for the first two sessions were

Daniel Willingham and Kate Jones. This worked well, further building on the existing knowledge, expertise and confidence of staff in this area.

Introducing retrieval practice to students

After the first CPD on the science of memory had been delivered to staff they had begun to integrate this within their practice. The next step was to share this with our students.

We introduced the importance of memory to students through a series of assemblies to the whole school explaining the basics of memory and how everybody can remember things better. We were able to link this with their understanding of growth mindset and the habits of mind. We explained to children that after we learn something, we don't forget it but actually it is in our long-term memory, and we have to improve the retrieval strength of the memory so we can use and apply the knowledge. We use the analogy that Clare Sealey suggested of the pesky knowledge playing hide and seek. The children's job is to find the knowledge and the more often they try to find it and the harder it can be to find, the better they will remember it next time.

Clare suggested explaining to the children that if they are the 'seeker' in hide and seek and they only count to five, they may find the other children quickly but their seeking skills won't be tested and developed. However, if they are a seeker who counts to 50, it will be much harder to find the other children but they will really develop their skills of seeking and be a much better seeker in future. This is a great way to help younger children understand the basis of the forgetting curve and deal with their frustrations if they cannot remember something and are being prompted to try to remember it rather than being immediately retaught or being allowed to look back at their notes. Teachers reinforced this within the classroom and would explicitly refer to memory within their lessons. They would speak to the children and point out when we were doing retrieval practice and remind them why.

As part of the action research, one group within school began focusing on salient knowledge. We share the learning intention with the children and speak through why they are learning what they are learning and how it fits into a sequence. We wanted to take it a step further than that and ensure children really understood what the key knowledge was they were being taught. The salient knowledge action research group piloted a way in which children could self-reflect at the end of each lesson. Previously, children reflected by using the success criteria to assess what went well and what their next steps were. Instead, the four teachers across key stages 1 and 2 trialled children reflecting on the salient knowledge of the lesson, alongside what went well. They reported finding that this encouraged them, as teachers, to more explicitly identify what the key knowledge was that they wanted the children to remember and resulted in more discussion in class about the key knowledge the children had learned. This knowledge was directly linked to the knowledge bank and was used for retrieval practice the next day as well as incorporated into low stakes quizzes.

The children being active agents in their learning is important to us as we strive to ensure all children become independent life-long learners and transform their own life chances. Therefore, teaching meta-cognitive skills is at the heart of what we do. Part of our commitment to this includes encouraging children to be their best self. A journal was created first by Carley Dawkin, an art teacher in one of our secondary schools, which I then developed for primary schools. This journal provides an opportunity for students to reflect weekly on their learning, alongside a weekly activity where children are explicitly taught meta-cognitive and self-regulation strategies.

In foundation stage and key stage 1, there is more focus on verbal discussions and students complete a big A3 journal whereas in key stage 2, all children have their own A5 sized journals which they keep in their trays and can refer to in all lessons. As we have focused more on incorporating research on memory into our practice, we have developed the journals so the 2022-2023 version includes explicitly the teaching of meta-memory skills.

Within the journal's weekly reflection page, children write down three pieces of salient knowledge they have learned that week to encourage them to retrieve information (you can see how explicitly mentioning this in lessons really helped the children to identify it). In the weekly activities, children are explicitly taught retrieval strategies and given the opportunities in their journals to write their own low stakes quizzes, use white boards to test their partners, use their knowledge banks to test each other, use braindumps, make flash cards and various other techniques. Most importantly, they are given a basic understanding of why these techniques work which means they have become more purposeful. I have heard Kate say about how often students get to Year 10 or 11 and they start to be taught revision strategies and it's new to them whereas if they had been taught it earlier, it would become a habit. This is exactly what I tell my children. By learning these techniques now and understanding how their memory works and how to improve the retrieval strength of their memories, they're ahead of the game.

Introducing retrieval practice to parents and carers

The next stakeholder group we needed to consider were parents and carers. Firstly, we focused on improving our communication with families about our curriculum and the key knowledge we wanted the children to learn in general. We started to send out Microsoft Sways at the start of each term which explained what the children would learn the following term. This was a document that parents could refer back to throughout the term so they were fully informed of what their children were learning. The knowledge banks are available on the school website to access and a weekly newsletter is sent home.

In our newsletter, we share what each year group is doing that week and a different curriculum area is focused on each week. One of our curriculum areas, which weaves throughout our curriculum, is 'thinking about thinking' which includes the 'be your best self' journal, meta-cognition and meta-memory. We also started to use the online platform 'Seesaw'. This allowed parents to have a more direct link to the teachers and also to see some of the learning occurring within the classroom and the children's homework. All these methods started to develop our contact with parents around the curriculum with the aim being to promote regular retrieval practice at home.

By explicitly making all homework retrieval practice, this was our parents'/carers' introduction to retrieval. Teachers sent announcements to parents on Seesaw to explain that we would be focusing purely on retrieval for homework, what this meant and why. In years 4, 5, 6, we are trialling using the Carousel learning platform for homework. Once we had introduced Carousel to children in assembly and explained to them why we would be using it, we sent an announcement to parents on Seesaw explaining the change to homework, referring again to the effectiveness of retrieval practice for enhancing retrieval strength.

During my parents' meetings this term, I spoke to the parents about homework. Some explained it has reduced the stress of homework as the answers are there which takes the pressure off them as parents. Now their child completes homework more independently or, if they do still require support, they no longer have to try and explain things to their child who is adamant they have never learned the topic before and can't do it. The parent knows the child has learned it and if they cannot remember, they can use the flashcards to revise. Some parents also mentioned that they can see how the quizzing has helped their child to recall things quicker and have shared that they are watching them complete the homework and then verbally quizzing them on the questions, or similar in the car or on the walk to school to provide further retrieval practice. This has helped parents see for themselves the benefits of retrieval. Beyond homework, just as we encouraged teachers to talk about memory explicitly with the children, we encouraged them to explicitly talk about memory with the parents too.

At this point, we decided that we needed to be more explicit with parents about retrieval practice. To further engage parents, we sent out Kate's video on retrieval practice for parents, available on her YouTube channel, as a whole school announcement with an explanation of why we do retrieval and how it works along with some suggestions for retrieval practice at home.

Our next step is a workshop for parents and carers on retrieval techniques where they can come into school and take part in an interactive workshop with their children. I would like to invite parents into lessons where they can see their children engaging in retrieval practice. Eventually, the 'be your best self' journals will become digital as we move towards one-to-one devices, and this will be a brilliant way that children can share their reflections and the salient knowledge they've learned with their parents.

We are considering how we anchor this change and are working on ensuring that we continue to develop our practice, embed our new policies and ensure new staff members who join the school learn about the science of memory and retrieval. We will continue to monitor and reflect on our practice, learning from colleagues within our academy and beyond to ensure retrieval practice is part of our puzzle of teaching and learning and is here to stay.

Thank you to Ella Martin for sharing all that she has done, alongside her colleagues, to promote retrieval practice across the whole school community. I have discovered a lot from Ella, about how retrieval practice can be effectively implemented and embedded across a primary school and a multi-academy trust. You can follow Ella on Twitter @ellamartin_ks2.

My main piece of advice is to talk about retrieval practice. I encourage schools to use that specific terminology too, as it becomes part of a common shared language with teachers, students and families. Talk to colleagues about retrieval practice tasks that have or haven't worked well in the classroom. Discuss research and reflect during meetings and insets. In the classroom talk to students about retrieval practice, including the benefits and how it is helping their learning; hopefully in time they will see this for themselves too.

During parents' evenings and open evenings refer to retrieval practice, include it in written reports and seize opportunities to share this powerful and effective strategy within your school community. It can lead to students developing evidence-informed and effective study that will benefit them when they leave primary school and enable them to become successful lifelong learners.

As a secondary specialist this process has made me think deeply and reflect on key stage 3 curriculum design. At secondary school some subjects rely heavily on students arriving with existing knowledge and skills whereas other topics and subjects can be treated as a blank slate (to an extent). Spending so much time in primary classrooms and talking to students I realised I should aim to be far more ambitious and challenging with both curriculum design and lesson planning in the future with KS3.

I have worked in two all through schools and with hindsight I should have worked more closely with my primary colleagues and spent more time in the primary classrooms. This is difficult to make a reality, not just because of the disruption and isolation due to the pandemic which made visiting other classes impossible or challenging, but mainly due to time. Time is often one of the biggest barriers teachers face when it comes to the development of curriculum or professional learning.

Teachers and leaders across phases and key stages should communicate often about learning, as should teachers working with students during the transition from primary to secondary. Cognitive psychology findings from the study of human memory tell us that in terms of memory and how people of all ages learn there is more in common across learners than we realise. However, it is important to show appreciation, awareness and respect for the unique differences across key stages, subjects and school contexts.

Primary schools are not mini secondary schools so trying to shoehorn secondary style tasks and activities into a primary classroom simply won't work and teachers at primary know this. Primary teachers have a special and in-depth knowledge of their classes, especially as so much time is spent with their students during an academic year. This is and always will be the greatest asset in terms of effectively implementing and embedding retrieval practice in the primary classroom.

Further recommended reading

An Ethic of Excellence: Building a Culture of Craftsmanship with Students. Ron Berger. (2003)

Understanding How We Learn: A Visual Guide. Yana Weinstein and Megan Sumeracki with Oliver Caviglioli. (2018)

How Can I Remember All That? Simple Stuff to Improve Your Working Memory. Dr Tracy Packiam Alloway. (2019)

A Parent's Guide to Powerful Teaching. Patrice Bain. (2020)

ACKNOWLEDGEMENTS

This is always difficult because there are too many people to include and thank! Firstly, I want to thank all those who have contributed case studies to this book. There were gaps in my knowledge and experience that people with expertise were able to enhance. I am very grateful to Shannen Doherty, Neil Almond, Lekha Sharma, Adam Woodward, Aidan Severs, Ceridwen Eccles and the staff at Jerry Clay Academy for sharing their experience, expertise and wisdom in this book. I am also very grateful to Clare Sealy for writing the foreword as Clare was my first choice and I was thrilled when she agreed to do so!

A huge thank you to all the primary teachers and school leaders who took time out of their busy schedules to talk to me or invite me to their school. This has helped me write and shape this book. There are far too many to name but a special thank you to Ysgol Rhoscolyn and The Thinking Schools Academy Trust (TSAT).

I am continually learning about retrieval practice and will continue to do so in the future. I would like to thank Professors Robert and Elizabeth Bjork. Despite their busy schedule, the distance between us and different time zones they are always willing to help and support me. A huge thank you to Bob Bjork for checking the accuracy of the research with my evidence-informed curriculum design plan. They are the world leading experts on human memory and I am incredibly lucky to be able to seek their advice and help.

Other academics I wish to thank include Professor John Dunlosky, Professor John Hattie, Professor Pooja K. Agarwal, Professor Alan Baddeley and of course, Professor Paul A. Kirschner. I owe a lot to Dylan Wiliam, as all teachers do, because he has contributed so much to moving the teaching profession forward and his knowledge of memory, teaching and learning is phenomenal.

There are many people in the teaching community I wish to thank. All of my former colleagues, again too many to name. Louise Rycroft, as she sparked my interest in memory and introduced me to a field that I have become fascinated by, in addition to being a great friend to me. There are lots of educators from Twitter I am grateful for and learn from continually. Thank you to Patrice Bain, Blake Harvard, Rachel Ball, Adam Boxer, Tom Sherrington, Oliver Caviglioli, Robin Macpherson,

Kristian Still, Jon Hutchinson, Nathan Gynne, Sinéad Moxham, Sara Wyn Roberts, Simon Smith and Dan Morrow.

The team at John Catt Publishing, especially Alex Sharratt, Jonathan Barnes, Meena Ameen and Peter Douglas, who continue to support me and publish my books! Thank you!

Finally and most importantly, my family. Thank you for your support and love.

QR CODES

 This is my TES resources homepage. Here you can download templates to all my retrieval practice resources, for free. There is also a guide I created for parents and carers about retrieval practice in primary.

 This QR code will direct you to https://www.carousel-learning.com/.

 This QR code will direct you to the Education Endowment Foundation (EEF) homepage.

 This QR code will direct you to the Evidence Based Education homepage.

This QR code will direct you to the website created by the 'Learning Scientists' who share evidence-informed strategies with teachers, students and parents.

The Early Career Framework (ECF).

Ofsted Education Inspection Framework (2019).

This QR code will take you to a video explanation of 'The Leitner System' by Jon Hutchinson.

 This QR code will take you to https://www.
retrievalpractice.org/ created by Professor
Pooja K. Agarwal. The website contains blogs,
resources, links to research and free guides to
download.

ALSO AVAILABLE IN THE RETRIEVAL PRACTICE COLLECTION:

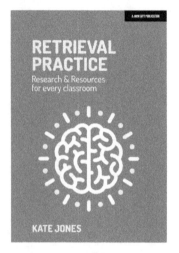

ISBN: 9781912906581   £10

ISBN: 9781913622411   £10

ISBN: 9781913622541   £8

CPSIA information can be obtained
at www.ICGtesting.com
Printed in the USA
JSHW052000290722
28599JS00003B/3